SAVING PLANTS
AND JOBS

Union-Management
Negotiations
in the Context
of Threatened
Plant
Closing

Paul F. Gerhart
Case Western Reserve University

1987

W. E. Upjohn Institute for Employment Research

Library of Congress Cataloging-in-Publication Data

Gerhart, Paul F.
  Saving plants and jobs.

  1. Plant shutdowns. I. Title.
  HD5708.5.G47 1987   331.89'15   87-10527
  ISBN 0-88099-047-3
  ISBN 0-88099-046-5 (pbk.)

THE INSTITUTE, a nonprofit research organization, was established on
July 1, 1945. It is an activity of the W. E. Upjohn Unemployment Trustee
Corporation, which was formed in 1932 to administer a fund set aside by
the late Dr. W. E. Upjohn for the purpose of carrying on ''research into
the causes and effects of unemployment and measures for the alleviation
of unemployment.''

ii

iii

Acknowledgments

A project like this could not be completed without the cooperation of the union and management representatives who agreed to be interviewed. These individuals, in addition to being interviewed, agreed to review portions of the manuscript to which they contributed. To these individuals, who in fact wrote this book, I express whole-hearted thanks.

Special thanks are also due to Bill Otten, who worked diligently as project research assistant during its early stages. Bill was instrumental in many of the union contacts and conducted a number of the interviews. My secretary, Fran Snyder, also deserves special thanks for putting the manuscript into final form.

Finally, the financial support of the Upjohn Institute is gratefully acknowledged, along with the patience of Wayne Wendling and Allan Hunt of the Institute staff.

The Author

Paul F. Gerhart has been a faculty member in the Weatherhead School of Management, Case Western Reserve University, Cleveland, Ohio since 1977. He received his Ph.D. from the University of Chicago. Professor Gerhart was a faculty member at the Institute of Labor and Industrial Relations, University of Illinois, and visiting assistant professor at the University of Chicago before coming to CWRU. More recently, he has held positions as visiting professor at the University of Glasgow, Scotland and as visiting research scholar at the Swedish Center for Working Life in Stockholm.

Professor Gerhart's other research interests include public sector collective bargaining, dispute resolution procedures, and institutional aspects of wage determination. He is also an active labor arbitrator.

Contents

Introduction

Plant closings are a lot like funerals. Objectively, we all have to die—dying is part of life—and as the sermon usually goes, death gives rise to new life. Economists have argued in their dispassionate, objective fashion that plant closure is simply the other side of opening new plants and that the mobility of physical resources adds vitality to an economy, which in turn helps promote the general welfare. Plant closing is not always a good thing, however, and no one would be foolish enough to argue that. Both death and plant closings can sometimes be prevented. "Premature" plant closings are a social waste and a terrible personal tragedy to those directly affected. Any shutdown of a manufacturing or service facility has significant private and social consequences as human resources are displaced. Plant closure is all the worse when it could have been avoided.

Research on the problem of plant closure has taken two directions. The first is to measure and describe the consequences of decisions to close.[1] The second relates to the alternative courses of action available to government, employees, and employers to ameliorate these consequences with the more sophisticated research attempting to evaluate these alternatives.[2] Understanding the consequences of closure and evaluating alternatives to deal with it are important, but recently McKersie & McKersie have suggested, "the best way to deal with potential job loss is to prevent it if this can be done by some sensible basis."[3] Unfortunately, aside from the McKersie & McKersie report, few research findings on the issue of closure prevention are available.[4] How can plant closing be prevented? Which cases are "preventable"? Why aren't the necessary preventive steps always taken? Why are they taken in some cases? These are the questions addressed in this study.

Scope and Outline of the Study

This study is not about the preservation of plants and jobs that are no longer economically viable. Rather it is about *why* plants get that way and how to prevent it from happening prematurely. To understand why Cleveland's "anchor industries" were declining and why its jobs were being located elsewhere, the McKinsey and Company staff for the Cleveland Tomorrow Committee interviewed chief executives, conducted case studies, and surveyed trade literature concerning these in-

1

dustries. The three critical factors they identified in Cleveland's decline were high union labor costs, increased foreign competition and low capital investment. With respect to union labor costs, the report cited above average wage rates in Cleveland, restrictive work rules and the legacy of poor labor-management relations.[5]

Chapter 1 of this study analyzes the causes for a plant's loss of economic viability, recognizes that labor factors are only part of the equation, and raises a series of questions about short- and long-run phenomena that impinge on the plant closing decision.

Chapter 2 describes several plant closures in Northeast Ohio. Declining markets, increased competition from more efficient producers, and obsolete facilities were the proximate causes for closure in the three cases discussed. High labor costs and a "poor labor climate" had a bearing but were not the immediate cause for closure. These cases form a backdrop for understanding plant closure and illustrate the complexity of the process. The major lesson of chapter 2 is that closure is not the result of one simple, "point-in-time" decision. Rather, closure results from a series of earlier events and decisions in which local decision-makers, managers and union representatives have often played a significant role. At least two of the closures discussed in chapter 2 may well be viewed as "the legacy of a poor labor climate."

Chapter 3 reviews four cases in which labor relations issues played a direct part in the threatened closure. These cases show that not all labor-management relationships are hopelessly combative, however. In all four cases, work rule changes significantly reduced labor costs, and improved labor-management relations promise productivity improvement in the future. In economic terms, these firms have found it more cost effective to invest in a reversal of their combative labor-management relationship than to exit the area.

As this study progressed and tentative conclusions were reached, it became clear that cases involving explicit threats of closure represented only the potential failures in the process of preserving plants and jobs. Limiting the study to them would be like studying collective bargaining by looking only at cases where strikes had occurred. Chapter 4 remedies this shortcoming by introducing two cases where no explicit threat to close was made, but the implications for job security of a failure to act were clear to all. Both cases involve decisions to locate new facilities in close proximity to existing plants whose state of obsolescence was progressing rapidly. Thus, chapter 4 is really about bargaining for job security with a long-term perspective as much as it is about saving jobs that are threatened by a near-term plant closure.

Chapter 5 summarizes the findings of the earlier chapters and suggests some public and private policy conclusions. Although definitive answers do not come from a study of this kind, it is perhaps more important that people concerned with the issues posed here ask the right questions. If this report achieves that much it will have been a success.

NOTES

1. For discussions of these consequences, see for example James L.Stern, "Consequences of Plant Closure," *Journal of Human Resources*, VII, 1 (Winter 1972) pp. 3-12; Robert L. Aronson and Robert B. McKersie, *Final Report: Economic Consequences of Plant Shut-downs in New York State*, New York State School of Industrial and Labor Relations, Cornell University, May 1980, pp. iii-x, 1-171; Barry Bluestone and Bennett Harrison, *The Deindustrialization of America* (New York: Basic Books, 1982); Hearings U.S. Senate, September 1980; John Hughes, *Industrial Restructuring: Some Manpower Aspects*, Discussion paper No. 4, National Economic Development Office, Millbank, London, May 1976; Stephen S. Mick, "Social and Personnel Costs of Plant Shutdowns," *Industrial Relations* 14 (May 1975) pp. 203-208; Jeanne P. Gordus, Paul Jarley, and Louis A. Ferman, *Plant Closings and Economic Dislocation* (Kalamazoo, MI: W. E. Upjohn Institute for Employment Research, 1981).

2. See for example Robert B. McKersie and Werner Sengenberger, *Job Losses in Major Industries: Manpower Strategy Responses*, Organization for Economic Cooperation and Development, Paris, 1983.

3. Robert B. McKersie and William S. McKersie, *Plant Closings: What Can Be Learned from Best Practice* (Washington, DC: Government Printing Office, 1981, p. 4).

4. See Wayne R. Wendling, *The Plant Closure Policy Dilemma* (Kalamazoo, MI: W. E. Upjohn Institute for Employment Research, 1984) for a discussion of the potential role of collective bargaining in saving plants and the public policy alternatives associated with such a role.

5. *Cleveland Tomorrow—A Strategy for Economic Vitality*, Cleveland Tomorrow Committee, December 1981, pp. 5-6.

1

The Economics of Plant Closure
Some Research Questions

The economist offers a simple answer to the question of why a particular plant closed—it was no longer profitable. A slightly more complex version is that the profitability of the plant fell below a minimal threshold level for the company so that an alternative investment of the capital embodied in the plant was preferable to continued operation. Such economic explanations are helpful in focusing on the problem, but they do not begin to answer the next question—*why* is the plant no longer profitable? Why is the plant "uncompetitive"? Why has it not been "modernized"? Why are labor or other factor costs higher than elsewhere, or why did demand fall? These questions require an institutional examination of the *ceterus* considered by economic theory to be *paribus*.

In particular, this study focuses on the labor factor and its relative importance in decisions to close plants. Other factors cannot be ignored and there is no intention in this study of sweeping them under the rug or suggesting that if all the labor factor issues could be resolved, plants would go on forever. Such a conclusion is simply not true. The labor factor has been identified as a key element in the competitiveness of particular areas, however, so it is fair to attempt an evaluation of the role of that factor despite a recognition that other factors affecting the viability of a particular plant may overwhelm the labor element.

Response to Change

Among the factors economists identify as contributors to a plant's decline is its inability to respond to external changes in product and factor markets or to internal opportunities for technological advancement.

Short-Run Changes in the Product Market

The simplest example of a need for change may be the case where new competitors erode the monopoly power of particular producers and

5

force a decline in market price. To the extent that employees have shared in the monopoly rents (profits) with their employer, there will necessarily be a downward adjustment in labor costs, either through a more efficient utilization of labor or direct reduction of wages and benefits, if the plant is to survive. "Concession bargaining" demonstrates that downward adjustments are sometimes made. Such negotiations are always difficult, in part, for reasons outlined in figure 1.1. The following paragraph numbers correspond to the numbers in the Plant Closing Negotiation Model.

1. Two kinds of employer motivation give rise to the possibility of plant closing negotiations. A *bona fide* (1A) motivation is one where the employer actually considers closing for reasons which may or may not be related to the labor climate. Alternatively, an employer may use the threat of plant closing as a bluff (1B) in an effort to gain bargaining leverage.

To the external observer, including union leaders, distinguishing between these two motivations may be difficult. Many employees believed during the recession of the early 1980s that their company was taking advantage of the economic times. With other plants closing, however, any threat had to be taken seriously.[1] The appropriate response is obviously different in the two situations. A wrong conclusion—for example, that (1B) exists when in fact (1A) is the case—may be fatal. How do unions distinguish? Are they now aware of mistakes they have made in the past?

2. Given that an employer has a *bona fide* motivation, it may proceed with an analysis of its operations, make a firm decision to close its facilities, and then announce this decision to its employees and their union (2A); or the employer may raise the matter for discussion with its employees, perhaps by suggesting areas where labor cost considerations have a bearing on its closing decision (2B). When does an employer initiate such discussions? Why? Under what circumstances does the employer simply make the decision with no attempt to adjust labor cost factors through discussions with the union?

2.1. The Supreme Court, federal circuit courts, and the National Labor Relations Board (NLRB) have issued a number of decisions concerning the employer's legal obligation to negotiate when a decision is made to subcontract, close down facilities completely, or partially shut down facilities. In *First National Maintenance*[2], The Supreme Court determined that a firm was obligated to negotiate the impact or effect of its

Figure 1
Plant Closing Negotiations Model

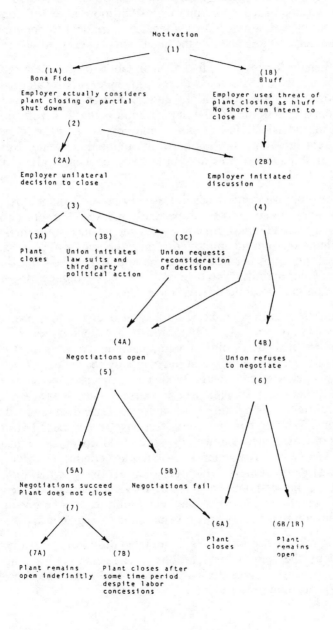

decision to reduce its operations, but not to negotiate with respect to the actual decision. In 1981, the International Union of Electrical Workers sued Singer for closing a plant in Newark, New Jersey. Pantry Pride was also sued by its unions in Baltimore after the company closed a number of stores.[3] Does a legal requirement to negotiate, or the threat of legal action, enhance the likelihood of success in saving jobs?

2.2. When an employer has had difficult labor-management relations and has generally faced a union the employer feels is recalcitrant and uncompromising, does that employer seek to avoid any contact with the union and thus minimize the unpleasantness that is involved in the plant closing decision? The employer may expect that the longer the union is kept ignorant, the less harm the union can create. In short, what, if anything, motivates an employer to conceal a plant closure decision?

2.3. The employer who raises the issue of possible plant closing for discussion may do so out of a hope that concessions might be made or out of a loyalty to long-term employees and a concern for their well-being. What motivates an employer to raise the matter of plant closing is a critical question, because unless the employer raises the issue in a timely manner and offers to discuss it, there is a reduced likelihood that anything can be done to save the plant.

3. When an employer makes a unilateral decision to close, union leaders may not respond at all (3A); they may respond by initiating law suits or other third party political action designed to forestall the closing (3B); or they may request that the company reconsider its decision and offer to discuss some of the labor cost aspects associated with it (3C). The 3B and 3C responses may of course be combined where union leaders are merely using the 3B response to gain leverage in the 3C negotiations. Why is there no union response sometimes? Is it a lack of interest or expertise to deal with the issues? Do leaders view the situation as a lost cause? Do general labor market conditions affect their response? How do leaders decide between 3B or 3C when they take action? Is 3C the response most likely to yield success—to keep the plant open indefinitely? If it is, how can union leaders be encouraged to take that alternative? What prevents their taking that approach?

4. Union response to an employer-initiated discussion is likely to be motivated by the same considerations as a response to a unilateral employer decision to close. Research questions 3 and 4 are, therefore, closely related though not identical.

When an employer initiates a discussion of labor costs, union leader reaction may be favorable so that negotiations are undertaken (4A), or negative so that no discussions are undertaken (4B). The employer initiative might also be treated in a perfunctory way so that no real negotiations occur. Union leaders may take a negative position on reopening negotiations for strategic reasons related to the union's position in other bargaining units. For example, a refusal to meet might be motivated by concern for the pattern-setting effect any concessions might have. How important is this motive as a bar to negotiations on labor cost factors?

5. Perhaps the most important question in this study is what distinguishes successful (5A) from unsuccessful (5B) negotiations, once the parties are at the table. Successful negotiations are, of course, defined as those which maintain the plant.[4] When talks fail, is there generally a miscalculation on the part of the union concerning employer motivation (1A versus 1B)? That is, does the union conclude that the employer is bluffing when it is not? What other factors contribute to the failure of talks? What are the factors which lead to successful talks? Is it expertise and knowledge on the part of union negotiators concerning the economics of the situation the plant faces? When do employers or unions take a hard line in negotiations? Are their positions solely dependent on economic factors, or are leadership styles, personality variables, or other "nonrational" issues important to the outcome?

6. Where a union refuses to negotiate after a request from the employer (4B), either the employer closes the plant (6A) or the plant remains open (6B). When the latter happens, is it always safe to assume the employer was bluffing?

7. Finally, with respect to figure 1.1, is there a distinction between plants which remain open indefinitely (7A) and those which subsequently close anyway (7B), even though substantial labor cost concessions have been granted? Is it true that once concessions are requested it is usually too late to save the plant? Many union negotiators are not convinced that concessions save plants.[5]

Long-Run Changes—a "Tragedy Scenario"[6]

One model for an Elizabethan tragedy calls for the introduction of the hero's dilemma in the first and second acts, a set of events leading to a climax (the "handwriting on the wall") in the third act, and the playing out of the inevitable tragic conclusion in the fourth and fifth acts. Even though this model may reflect poetic license, and not a very good fit with the actual plays of Shakespeare, it does describe a pattern that applies to some production facilities in Cleveland.

Perhaps as long as 30 years before a particular plant is closed, corporate planners are called upon to expand facilities for increased output or new product lines. At that point in time, a decision is made to begin operations at an altogether new location. A variety of reasons is given for choosing a new location rather than expanding at the existing plant. Typically, they include availability of space at much lower cost, proximity to new or expanding markets or to suppliers, and occasionally matters related to labor and human resources. Avoidance of a militant union might be a factor, but this is often offset by the lack of a trained or trainable labor force, particularly in industries where there is special reliance on experienced or skilled workers.

Though it was not intended and never recognized as such, the decision to expand production in an entirely new location may be the climax of Act III. It is not part of a conscious 25-30 year long-term policy to relocate the corporation to the Sun Belt, but it is the decision that determines the eventual fate of the older original plant location. Once a plant is established in a new location, expansion of that facility is often easier than at the old location because planners have anticipated such needs and purchased extra land in the initial new construction. After several years, productivity and labor costs in the new plant are more favorable than in the old plant because the newer plant was built and equipped with the latest technology. As one union interviewee on this project noted, "If they gave us the equipment those guys down South have, we could make [product] twice as good as they do and twice as fast! With the junk we have to work with it's a wonder we get anything out of this plant."

When the inevitable recession occurs, production cutbacks are ordinarily scheduled for plants with the highest costs and lowest rates of productivity. If production is permanently reduced, "consolidation" or "rationalization" of production is concentrated into the more productive plants. Over a period of years, with successive expansions and contractions, the inevitable decision is made to close the old site completely. The only way to reverse such a process is via a new decision, sometime prior to the ultimate phase-out, to introduce new products or technology into the old plant. Such a decision can be made only when relative cost advantages dictate it.

Need for continuous change. In the long run, all markets change. Consumer tastes, customer needs, factor markets, and technological changes combine to assure that practically no product has an infinite life. In many plants, the products produced and the technology in use change, thus extending the life of the plant. In some plants, they do not. In view of limited product life cycles, change is the *sine qua non* for remaining viable. Part of the explanation for differences among plants is the perception on the part of management concerning the ease with which change could be introduced. A labor force that is thought to be rigid or unwilling to accept change would clearly stand as a "cost" in the evaluation of whether change should be introduced. Such a cost is just as surely an element in plant closing as "excessive wages." In fact, it may be a more serious issue because its effects are insidious and irreversible after some crucial point.

In this study, an attempt has been made to evaluate the relative importance of "labor force rigidity" as a factor contributing to the failure to introduce timely investment that could preserve plants and jobs. The research question is to what extent employee or union rigidity inhibits or eliminates the flexibility that is necessary to sustain a plant. Anticipating some of the study's findings, this question has been expanded to look into the extent to which unions actually seek or pursue change in product mix or technology in an effort to assure job security.

Greenfields closer to home. A good strategy for averting the tragedy scenario altogether was demonstrated in two cases reported in chapter 4. Instead of relocating a new facility to an altogether different area of the country, new "greenfield" plants were built in close proximity (easy commuting distance) to the existing plant. New technologies and the scope of the expansion projects demanded new plants, but contrary to the usual tragedy scenario, these plants were built nearby, despite the fact that more distant locations were seriously considered by management. Union leaders were called upon to make contract modifications to accommodate the new plants, not only with respect to the conditions and benefits of the yet-to-be-hired employees, but also for existing employees.

Why do some union leaders comprehend the importance of plant location decisions and make the effort to influence them? When does management recognize the possibility of improving its *overall* relationship with the union and take the risk of negotiating a matter that is clearly beyond the purview of the NLRA's mandatory scope of bargaining? What factors contribute to the successful conclusion of such negotiations?

Personalities and "Politics"

Rank-and-file resistance and union politics have also been cited as a key factor in determining the success of negotiations when employers ask for concessions. Such considerations may determine whether path 4A or 4B is followed in figure 1.1. Thomas Miner, vice-president of labor relations for Chrysler was quoted recently on this. "Industry's problems at the bargaining table are not now with union leadership, but with the rank-and-file."[7]

The leadership on both sides of the labor-management relationship appears to play crucial roles in determining whether particular plants survive. Even leaders with Messianic traits cannot step into a situation that lacks economic viability and save it. As noted above, this study is not about such situations. Rather, this research question concerns plants that appear to be economically viable, but ineffective leadership causes premature closure. More broadly, the research question relates to the importance of leadership and other noneconomic elements in determining whether plants close prematurely. Why is it that union members vote to reject concessions despite the fact that job loss will follow? Why does such behavior, which appears irrational from an economic standpoint, occur?

Summary

An underlying premise in this study has been that plants that have lost their economic viability will be closed. No heroic effort will save them. Many plants close prematurely, however. The most visible situation involving premature closure is one where relatively short-run changes in product market competition erode the monopoly rents of an employer and require the downward adjustment of wages. Convincing a union, and more important its constituents, that such adjustments are necessary, is the crucial step in saving a plant in this situation. How does that process work?

Cases where longer term change has not been accommodated are less visible. That is, the closure seems inevitable when it occurs, but to those who review the situation carefully, it is evident that actions could have been taken to extend the life of the plant had they been undertaken early enough. New products and investment in new processes are crucial throughout a plant's life. The key question here is why such actions were not taken in a timely fashion.

Finally, noneconomic contributing elements cannot be dismissed. How important are they in situations where potentially viable plants fail? Are there systematic explanations for the failure of interpersonal or political relationships?

The following chapters provide case examples that illustrate some of the issues raised in this chapter. They provide partial and tentative answers for some of the questions. Some readers will disagree with the conclusions reported here. It is hoped that they will be inspired to offer their own conclusions or, better still, engage in their own research to better address the issues involved.

The usual caveat regarding the usefulness of case studies must be entered. They raise more questions than they answer in any definitive way.

NOTES

1. *Wall Street Journal,* October 13, 1982, p. 1.

2. *First National Maintenance Corporation v. National Labor Relations Board,* 452 US, 666 (1981).

3. *Wall Street Journal,* October 13, 1982, p. 16.

4. In the context of the ''Tragedy Scenario'' (see next section), even a partial shutdown could be seen as a failure of plant saving negotiations. Where plants are partially saved, however, there is still a chance for a ''comeback'' so each case of a partial shutdown or retention must be judged individually as to whether negotiations were a success.

5. *Wall Street Journal,* October 13, 1982, p. 16.

6. Thanks are due to Tommy McQuistion, former vice-president of Parker Hannifin and executive-in-residence at the Weatherhead School of Management, 1982-83, for first calling the pattern described in this section to the author's attention.

7. *Labor Relations Reporter, News and Background Information,* 112 LLR 326 (April 1983).

2
Why Plants Close

In any dynamic economy, capital investments must be retired at the end of their useful lives and replaced by more productive investments. The industrial structure and its geographic distribution respond to a variety of powerful economic forces, including changes in prices, consumer preferences, production technologies, and international trade competition. The opening of new plants and closing of obsolete plants are part of this vital process.[1]

Joseph Schumpeter noted in 1898 that the opening and closing of manufacturing facilities probably signifies economic health to the extent that they assist growth and competitiveness. A major premise for this study is that *bona fide* economic reasons lie behind virtually all plant closing decisions. In many cases, those reasons are beyond the control of local managers and other decisionmakers at the point when the decision to close is under consideration. As noted in the preceding chapter, however, if a longer-run perspective is used, the inevitability of closure at the point when it occurs is not always so obvious.

The three cases of this chapter illustrate this point in widely divergent ways. Some of the lessons to be learned from them are summarized at the conclusion of the chapter.

Blue Water Seafood

The Blue Water Seafood plant was located on the west side of Cleveland. Prior to its closure in 1979, it produced an "economy label" seafood fillet. Frozen fish, processed on board ship, were purchased by Blue Water, breaded, packaged and refrozen. Fish sticks and other forms of "fish portions" were distributed through food brokers to grocery outlets and the fast food trade.

The plant was built in 1964 by a Cleveland-based company that had outgrown its original location. Shortly afterward, Gorton, a Boston-

15

based national seafood distributor, purchased the Cleveland company and added the plant to its chain of plants in New England, Alabama and Canada. The plant had approximately 180 unskilled employees at that time who had been unionized by the Meat Cutters (United Food and Commercial Workers) in the late 1960s.

In 1975, Gorton was purchased by General Mills. Employment at the plant continued to grow until it reached about 300 employees in 1979. Labor relations at the time of the purchase in 1975 were characterized as poor by union and management interviewees. Both agreed, however, that relations improved substantially after a new manager was assigned by General Mills.

By 1979, the industry for food service fish portions was suffering from overcapacity, with little growth opportunity and intense price competition. A new market trend for frozen food had become apparent—economy frozen foods were being displaced by "up-market"products—so Cleveland plant products saw a gradual decline in demand. The result was very poor profit performance and return on investment in the Cleveland plant. For that reason, in mid-April 1979, General Mills decided to withdraw from large segments of the food service business which the Cleveland plant supplied. The plant was closed on May 31.

Employer Decision

In late 1978, General Mills began to produce what later became known as "light batter" products for the retail market. These products, including fish sticks, are of premium quality. At that time, the company also reviewed its production capabilities at its three seafood production plants in Massachusetts, Alabama and Cleveland. Although the Massachusetts plant was somewhat older, it was a much larger plant and offered the opportunity for consolidation and integration of operations. Moreover, it produced primarily for retail product distribution. The newer Alabama plant was the production location for a stuffed seafood product for which demand was strong. The Cleveland plant had neither the equipment nor the room to absorb production from the plants in Alabama and Massachusetts. Conversely, Alabama and Massachusetts had the capacity to absorb the entire output of the Cleveland plant in economy-labeled fish sticks.

In short, the state of the frozen food market—particularly for food service products such as those produced in Cleveland—dictated that the company reduce its production capacity. Cleveland, through a combination of factors, was the logical choice for closure. The Cleveland plant was "stuck" with the economy label product that was slowly being phased out by the company. The alternative sites had excess capacity or were experiencing increasing demand in "up-market products" that were compatible with the light batter products the company was about to introduce.

All interviewees agreed that labor relations, including labor costs and labor climate, were not a significant factor in the decision to close the Cleveland plant. Although there had been two earlier strikes in the plant, the labor relations climate had improved substantially between 1975 when General Mills acquired the plant and 1979 when the closure occurred. Hourly labor costs in Cleveland were the highest among the three plants, but the relatively small difference was not an important element in the company's decision to close the Cleveland plant.

Union Awareness/Decision Process

General Mills now has a policy of providing as much prenotification of closure or substantial layoff as possible to its unions and employees. In the case of the Cleveland plant closing, however, only about six weeks notice was given to the union. Although a concern for overcapacity and shifting demand in the product market had been expressed at corporate headquarters as much as a year earlier, a final decision to close the plant had been made very swiftly and was carried out expeditiously.

The union representative received a call in late April 1979 from the corporate industrial relations manager, who requested a meeting. When the union representative and his business agent arrived, the corporate representative simply announced that the plant would be closed on May 31. Union representatives were "stunned." They made several offers, including a six- or nine-year no-strike pledge, but the company representative indicated that the decision to close the plant was final. In management's view, lengthier discussions with the union would have been useless in this case since the decision to close the plant was unrelated to the labor relations climate or to anything within the control of the local union.

Further meetings between the parties were scheduled to discuss severance benefits and related matters, but nothing more was discussed concerning the decision to close. The plant did close on May 31, 1979 with the company meeting all its contractual obligations. The company also made efforts to find jobs for displaced employees. The state of the Cleveland labor market at the time, however, was so poor that little could be done to assist the employees.

Contributing Factors

The general labor relations climate at the plant had been good immediately prior to the closure. Four or five years earlier, however, at the time Gorton purchased the seafood processing company, relations were very poor. According to the union spokesperson, the replacement of the personnel manager at the plant by General Mills was a major step forward. Professional plant management had improved the performance of the plant and raised morale among the employees at the plant. There had been a strike in August 1976 that was inopportune from the union leadership's standpoint, since it occurred during the summer and covered a period when the plant was normally closed for summer vacations.

No "outsiders" were ever involved in an effort to save the plant. There was no external political pressure or assistance from the federal mediation service. In the union's view, there was no time to involve such people.

Perhaps the most important contributing factor in the closure was the state of the frozen food market—particularly for economy brand products such as those produced at the Cleveland plant. General Mills simply had excess capacity and needed to reduce it. The management spokesperson indicated that the entire industry was in difficult circumstances at the time and that other companies subsequently closed facilities after more substantial losses than General Mills had suffered in this case. By the expedited closure of this plant, the corporation was able to reduce losses, conserve capital, and position itself for a 1982-83 increase in demand which occurred among the up-market brands of products. In the management spokesperson's opinion, the right decisions by the company in a timely fashion in 1979 strengthened the corporation so that employees at other locations benefited. Unfortunately, the employees at the Cleveland location paid the price.

General Mills gave no thought to selling the facility to another producer of economy fish sticks or to some other manufacturer. The breading mix manufacturing plant, located at the same site, is still in operation. At the time of the closure, only 20 employees worked in the breading plant, but now there are about 50, and employment is expected to expand. Breading mixes have been profitable and their market has expanded. Customers include other food processors as well as General Mills. The company has been well ahead of the market in developing new types of breading mixes for light batter products so that its breading facility in Cleveland has been particularly competitive.

General Mills also never considered the Cleveland plant for the introduction of new products. Although there have been minor additions to existing facilities in other locations, the company has not added any new free-standing facilities since 1979, and there has been no opportunity to move a different product into the Cleveland plant.

Inferences

Perhaps the most important lesson from this case is that reliance on a single product, narrowly defined even to its quality identity, can have a fatal consequence for plants. The Cleveland plant had limited flexibility to adapt as its business climate became less profitable. Without versatility or planning to replace products as they become obsolete, it is not possible to save an otherwise productive facility. In this plant, concentration on one product may have contributed to the efficient processing of fish sticks, but the absence of versatility led to the demise of the plant when the market for its product declined.

The short time frame of advance notice to the union (six weeks) precluded a thoughtful consideration of alternatives for the plant, but it is not clear that a longer time frame would have been of benefit under the circumstances. A more aggressive strategy by the union to pursue either alternative products from the same corporation, or a demand that the plant be turned over to a manufacturer who could use it, might have been beneficial, however.[2]

Finally, the poor quality of industrial relations earlier in the plant's history, 1970-1975, cannot be overlooked. That phenomenon is addressed more directly below. Although it is purely speculative at this point, a better climate coupled with union pressure for more investment or product diversity could have altered the potential for saving the plant.

Custom Lumber Products[3]

Increased fuel and transport costs following the 1973 oil embargo led to the closing of another Cleveland plant in 1984. Custom Lumber Products, Inc., a Northeast Ohio sawmill, was purchased in 1969 to mill custom lumber products for Wood City, an Ohio chain of lumberyards. In 1971, Wood City decided to build a new mill with modern equipment and material handling facilities, along with substantial storage capacity. Although pre-cut lumber was available from southern and western suppliers, Custom Lumber offered unique services. For example, specialized chemical treatments could be applied to custom cut materials, all for very rapid delivery. Moreover, prior to the increase in transportation costs in 1973, it was more profitable for Wood City to produce its own customized products than to rely on the more limited lines available from distant suppliers.

Employees were unionized in the original plant purchased by Custom Lumber Products. Drivers and warehouse workers at Wood City retail outlets were also unionized by the same union. They were covered by a separate contract, however.

Custom Lumber Product's profitability suffered two sharp drops. Prior to the 1973 oil embargo, the company operated in the black, but this picture rapidly changed with increased gasoline prices. Transportation costs for raw materials being shipped to the plant soared and the profit margin fell to near zero. By 1983, southern (nonunion) mill competitors reported average wage costs as low as $5 per hour, while wages in the Ohio plant reached $9.50. Furthermore the company provided family medical care at the same time that most of its competitors limited their contribution for health insurance to employees only. Pension plan costs of 38 cents per hour also reduced competitiveness since other suppliers did not offer pension provisions. Finally, the 1982 recession and severe depression of the western and southern mill industry led to price cutting by competitors. The imputed price at which Custom Lumber Products sold its product to Wood City had to be cut in response, so Custom Lumber's margin fell below zero.

Naturally, Wood City wanted the plant to be profitable, but it would have settled for breaking even on a yearly basis. It tolerated zero profits because Custom Lumber provided customized processing services. When the margin went negative, the plant could not be sustained.

Employer Decision

Western and southern lumber mills can supply only standard cut lumber. This is a disadvantage since it limits the range of products Wood City can offer and reduces its ability to respond to the unique needs of customers. On the other hand, transportation costs for the finished products of those mills are lower than for those of Custom Lumber because all processing wastes have been removed before the lumber is shipped to Cleveland. Sawdust and scrap from milling is left behind. This practice reduces transportation costs by about 20 percent compared with products produced by Custom Lumber Products.

By late 1981, Custom Lumber had completed an analysis of relative costs pertaining to the plant in Ohio. The negative results of this analysis led management to consider closing the mill. The dilemma facing management was simple. On one hand, it could continue operations, have ready access to customized products and accept the fact that red ink would flow. On the other hand, management could close the plant, accept the loss of customized products and services, and order standardized cut lumber from a western mill. A third alternative, one that would avoid this dilemma completely, was to persuade the union to agree to concessions on wages and benefits, and thereby reduce labor costs.

Union Awareness

No information about the company's 1981 studies of mill performance or the dilemma facing management had been given to the union. However, the local union president was fully aware of economic difficulties in the lumber industry, so the specific problem at this mill came as no great surprise. In a letter to the local union in January 1982, the company declared that it would be unable to pay the cost-of-living adjustment due later that month. Management proposed to meet with the union to discuss the matter.

The local union in this case represented employees at a number of different companies, not only Custom Lumber and Wood City. The local union president was also a vice-president of the national union. He was aware of negotiations in other parts of the country. Other union leadership at the plant level, however, was not nearly so sensitive to the precariousness of the members' jobs. The plant manager noted the difference among the union leaders. He commented that the local president's "main interest was to keep the plant open and his members working." The manager followed that statement with the more critical claim that the plant's business agent was ill-prepared to represent his members. The business representative apparently had no appreciation for the economics of the industry in which his members worked.

Decision Process

In its January 1982 memo to the union, the company stated that it would not be able to pay the cost-of-living increase scheduled to go into effect that month. The plant manager expressed a willingness to meet with union officials. Prior to that meeting, the union sent its auditor into the mill to ascertain the financial status of the company. The company willingly permitted this inspection. The auditor's report indicated that the company was losing about one-tenth of a cent on every board foot of lumber in the plant. This report laid to rest any concern on the part of the union that the company's claim of an inability to pay was unfounded.

After receiving his auditor's report, the local union president was convinced that the plant would shut down unless the operations could break even on a consistent basis. He also understood that as the cost of operating continued to escalate, Wood City, which owned Custom Lumber Products, would be more inclined to eliminate customized milling as an uncompetitive and impractical business practice.

The union agreed to open negotiations with the company concerning this situation in late January 1982. During those negotiations, management sought an agreement on a wage freeze, including the cost-of-living allowance. The company also wanted to eliminate two personal leave days. The union, concerned that even concessions might not save the plant, demanded an improvement in the severance pay clause if the mill closed its doors permanently. Moreover, the union wanted Wood City to give qualified employees top hiring priority at its retail outlets if the mill went out of business.

During the course of the negotiations, the parties also discussed the introduction of a new product in the plant. Wood City was about to begin selling a product known as "prestwood," a product manufactured from sawdust that is combined with a glue and pressed into shelving material. Management expected a growth in demand for this product and believed that it would enhance overall profits at the plant. In part, this expectation led management to accept a settlement without insisting on wage cuts.

In September 1982, after seven months of negotiations, agreement was reached. The union agreed to a three-and-one-half-year freeze on wages, including the cost-of-living allowance and the elimination of two personal leave days. In return, union members were assured of a severance allowance in the event of plant closure. The company also agreed to the union's demand that qualified employees would receive hiring priority at Wood City if the mill ceased operation.

Contributing Factors

Although there was a change in plant management during the course of these negotiations, the incoming plant manager had participated in the negotiations from their inception, and there was no discontinuity in the process. Moreover, the incoming plant manager actually wore two hats—one as new plant manager and the other as vice-president for Wood City. For that reason, there was no difficulty coordinating management's position in negotiations. Management's clear objective throughout these negotiations was to reduce labor costs to a level sufficient to permit the plant to operate on a break-even basis. Specific changes necessary to achieve this objective were negotiable.

On the union side, the local president had substantial credibility among union members. The company's presentations of its own financial situation and descriptions of the wage and benefits programs of competitors apparently convinced the employees that modification of the contract was justifiable. When the contract was put before the membership for ratification, union leaders unanimously endorsed the changes. Ratification was never in doubt.

Union-management relations at the mill prior to 1982 were harmonious. Only three or four grievances had ever reached the third step of the grievance procedure, and there had never been an arbitration case at the mill. Grievance activity increased, however, immediately after the negotiation of the concession package in the latter part of 1982. Management's view was that employees regarded plant closure as inevitable, a factor which severely lowered their morale. Employees became more sensitive to changes being implemented by management and were more likely to file grievances. A union spokesman hypothesized that management was attempting to increase productivity by tightening its application of work rules and by demanding higher levels of output from individual employees. In this way, the company hoped to reduce unit costs. The company had settled without a wage cut, at a higher labor cost level than necessary for the plant to break even. As a result other cost cutting methods were necessary to achieve the operating performance that management demanded. In the final analysis, this approach did not work.

Final Outcome

On April 11, 1985, the company announced that it would be closing the mill. No particular reason, other than a continued loss on operations at the mill, was cited by the company. Management determined that neither the milling operation nor the storage facility were necessary for efficient operation. The continued depression of the lumber industry provided Wood City with buying opportunities that made it no longer practical to operate the mill in Ohio. After the closure, Wood City began to purchase lumber from mills in the West, and products were delivered directly to individual retail outlets. Advances in inventory control technology eliminated the need for warehouse storage facilities.

Inferences

Building the mill was predicated on management's expectations about transportation and relative labor costs. When these expectations were not met, the mill became unprofitable.

In retrospect, it is unclear that *any* corrective action could have been taken to assure the future of this plant. As in the case of Blue Water Seafood, it is apparent that a limited-purpose facility such as this mill is risky for both management and employees. As soon as transportation costs altered the profit picture in 1973, the mill's future was in doubt. Perhaps if steps to change the product mix had been considered earlier, there would have been a greater chance for survival. In the 12-year period between 1973 and 1985, only one product, the "prestwood" project was introduced. It was "too little too late."

The union accepted all proposals by management for concessions. Despite that, in retrospect, the union might have done more. With the obvious advantage of hindsight, one can see that if the union had pressed for more product mix, the mill might have been more likely to survive. The only union request during 1983 negotiations was for an improvement in severance pay that was granted by management. In order to keep any plant open indefinitely, provision for the introduction of new products must be made. No such provision was made here, so closure was inevitable in the long run. The "long run" was considerably shortened by two factors: the sudden increase in energy prices in 1973 and the severe depression of the lumber industry of the 1980s.

Truck Components[4]

This truck parts plant had been the flagship of a Fortune 500 company from its post-World War I inception. After several major additions, the plant reached its peak employment with over 2,200 bargaining unit employees in the middle 1960s. Profitability at the plant began to decline by the mid-1970s as imports of foreign trucks and truck parts grew. The corporation and its competitors built facilities in the South and abroad to counter the import threat. These new facilities were in direct competition with the Cleveland plant.

A major decline in employment to 950 occurred in 1978 when the corporation moved the manufacture of heavy duty and off-road truck components to a new plant in the South. After that year, no new employees were hired at the plant. The recession further reduced employment to about 250 at the time the plant-saving negotiations began in January 1982.

Employer Decision

In May 1981, the corporation established a management task force to "look at what could be produced cheaper elsewhere." This review project came to be known as "Phase 3." Earlier projects known as Phase 1 and Phase 2 had involved the development of southern production facilities for the corporation and the movement of the heavy duty components line to the South. The goal of Phase 3 was to consider whether it was economically justifiable to consolidate all production and the prototype production facilities of the Cleveland plant into one of the existing southern locations. The complete closure of the Cleveland plant would follow. The principal focus of the investigation was on labor costs—wage rates and output per manhour. The southern plant used for comparison was unionized, but by a different international union. Although it was obvious that labor costs per unit of output were substantially lower at the southern facility, it was not clear that the difference would yield the *target* return on the investment cost of the move.

Union Awareness

The corporation made no effort to conceal its Phase 3 project. Informal discussions were held between Cleveland plant managers and union officials to let the latter group know about the corporate-level task force and the potential for Phase 3. This knowledge quickly reached the plant floor. The union was "desperate," according to a management spokesman. Hourly employment had dropped from approximately 2,200 people in 1967 to about 250 people at the time the Phase 3 news reached the floor. Although the recession had suppressed employment at the plant, maximum employment for the bargaining unit on the lines remaining in Cleveland could not exceed 450.

Bluffing was not part of management's strategy, nor did the union ever suspect that it was. Local management had a certain "face validity" because Phase 1 and Phase 2 had, in fact, been implemented with the loss of over half of the jobs at the Cleveland plant. Hence, there was no doubt among local union officials or the rank and file that Phase 3 was under consideration and would be implemented if economically justified.

Interviews with union negotiators substantiated the fact that they believed management's report on the Phase 3 study. There had been a substantial turnover of plant management in the past five to six years, but the plant manager who initiated the discussions had worked at the plant for over four years in various capacities. He was respected by the local union leadership and was believed to have considerable influence at the corporate level.

Decision Process

After a discussion with union leadership, the plant manager and his personnel director decided to undertake their own study of relative labor costs and the potential for saving the plant in Cleveland. They feared that if nothing were done prior to the release of the Phase 3 task force report, corporate management would make a decision based on that report without providing any opportunity for the local union in Cleveland to respond. Although the manager and personnel director undertook the study with the principal question being, "What will it take to save the Cleveland plant," they also saw their effort as related to the overall corporate objectives of maximizing profits. That is, if costs could be reduced at the Cleveland plant, the alternative of saving it was actually less expensive than moving to the South. Consequently, the corporation as a whole would benefit from preserving the plant in Cleveland.

On the basis of their studies, the plant manager and personnel director determined that a labor cost saving of approximately $5.00/hour would be necessary to retain the Cleveland facility. The local managers realized that employees at the Cleveland plant would not accept a $5.00/hour reduction in pay and benefits, even if it were necessary to save their jobs. The managers focused their attention on improving productivity, therefore, as a source of cost saving. Work rules which had evolved in the plant over its long history afforded them a great opportunity.

The local management team presented their views to corporate managers and received approval to open negotiations with the union in an effort to renegotiate the issues they had identified. These negotiations began in early January 1982. The parties faced a deadline of February 15, when the corporate capital allocation committee would decide whether to invest the necessary funds to make the move from Cleveland to the South.

An important part of management's strategy was to deal with union leaders rather than to attempt to bypass them with an appeal to the rank and file. In 1979, management had attempted to communicate directly with rank-and-file employees in the hope they could influence negotiators, but this technique was not successful at the bargaining table. It led to a 10-week stoppage. Since the union's leaders were firmly in control of the local union, leader support for the management proposals was a *sine qua non* for management's obtaining the labor cost changes necessary to forestall Phase 3.

At the initial meeting, the local management team presented the union with comparative labor cost and wage data. Comparisons were made with the wages and fringe benefits of the two principal domestic competitors of the corporation. Management also presented information on local Cleveland area wage surveys. The pattern of both sets of data showed that the employees in the corporation's plant at Cleveland had the best of all wage and benefit packages. Management asserted that if the Cleveland plant were to close, the alternative employment opportunities for union members were not appealing. Moreover, if wages and benefits were to "stand still" for even a few years, the employees would not be disadvantaged relative to others in their industry or occupations.

The union bargaining team, composed of local union representatives with one international business agent, was prepared to hear a demand for wage concessions. Instead, management proposed a reduction in future wage increases (which had already been negotiated) and the elimination of cost-of-living allowances. Management also proposed the reduction of four paid holidays per year and a modification in paid union time, an issue which had been critical in the 1979 negotiations. For local management, the most important aspect of the proposal was a list of work rule changes aimed at improving labor productivity and reducing labor costs through an increase in the "effort bargain." Specific details were omitted, but a general outline of the areas to be considered was laid on the table.

Following this first meeting, the union circulated the complete management proposal to the membership at the plant. In the opinion of local management, the fact that the company had not requested a wage roll back or significant benefit concessions strongly increased the likelihood of an early settlement with substantial labor cost savings through work rules modification.

Between January 6 and February 3, 1982, the company and the union held 13 meetings to negotiate the changes proposed by the company. On February 5 the union executive board voted 6 to 5 in favor of recommending the changes to the membership, and on February 11, 1982, the membership voted 176 to 82 to ratify the agreement. The most essential elements in this agreement from the company's viewpoint were modifications to work rules, flexibility in assignment, and the consolidation of job titles. The agreement to keep hourly labor costs constant over the term of the agreement (44 months) was also important. Although it was not part of the formal agreement, the company issued a "job security letter" that stipulated that with the approval of the agreement, the Phase 3 program would be "averted." The letter also guaranteed that employees with a seniority date prior to 1962 (existing employees currently active at work) would not be subject to layoff for the duration of the agreement.

The modifications to work rules comprised 21 pages of reference to contract clauses, side letters of agreement, and past practices that were eliminated or substantially modified. The practices included rules concerning assignment, premium pay, and job title consolidation.

Contributing Factors

The Cleveland plant was the original production facility in the corporation and had served as corporate headquarters until the mid-1960s. Many corporate executives had worked in the plant and in a sentimental way viewed the plant as the heart of the corporation, despite the fact that it no longer was. For that reason, proposals that could provide a rational justification for retaining the facility were welcomed at corporate headquarters.

As noted, there had been a substantial turnover in plant managers within this plant over the seven years prior to 1981. The plant manager in charge of the negotiations, however, had been employed at the plant since 1976, so that he was known to the union leadership. Moreover, he was thought to have substantial status within the corporate hierarchy and for that reason appeared to the union leaders to be able to speak with authority in these negotiations.

The union constituency in the Cleveland plant has historically been militant. The labor agreement never contained a clause for binding grievance arbitration, so grievances could be resolved through mid-contract strikes. These had occurred frequently at various times in the history of the relationship between the parties. Over the decade prior to 1982, however, union leaders and constituents had become less and less militant; there were no strikes in the plant after 1970. There was a 10-week lockout in 1979, when the company's position was "no agreement, no work."

The general climate of industrial relations in the plant was positive at the time of the interviews in 1982. The interpersonal relations between the union and the plant manager and plant industrial relations manager were good, although there had been some variation over the years due to the considerable turnover in these positions. Union-management meetings occurred on a regular basis, resulting in open communication. From the point of view of the corporation, the Cleveland plant historically had been the most militant in the truck component division, but this pattern had not been so clear between 1972 and 1982.

There was complete plant-level control over negotiations on the management side. On the union side, the international representative was present for negotiations, but the settlement was completely in the hands of local union leadership.

Final Outcome

Although the settlement agreement had achieved the efficiencies and economies sought by management, the state of the truck components markets served by this plant continued to decline throughout 1983. In addition, one of the company's domestic competitors came on line with a new production facility in the South, which substantially eroded the corporation's market in that area. In early January 1983, the corporation announced that it would have to reconsider the future of the Cleveland plant. Corporate spokespeople attributed the situation to the continuing recession, increased competition, and the deregulation of the trucking industry.

According to an article in the *Cleveland Plain Dealer* (January 12, 1983) management warned union officials about the potential for closing and the officials "were told to present alternatives to the closings." The corporation "did not say the Company was asking for concessions, leaving that decision to the [union]." Shortly thereafter, the union membership voted overwhelmingly to reject any further consideration of concessions. News reports indicated that union leaders and members felt betrayed. On January 27, 1983, the decision of the corporation to close the facility was made public.

Inferences

A *post hoc* analysis of this case shows that the Cleveland plant was the victim of the "tragedy scenario." The decision of the corporation to expand production facilities and move production lines to the South during the 1960s and 1970s clearly reduced the viability of the Cleveland plant. The new product lines and production technologies were introduced not in Cleveland, but in new plants in the South. When the economic crisis of the early 1980s occurred, the volume of production could not sustain all the plants the corporation had developed.

Moreover, the chairman of the corporation announced there were several other corporate objectives that influenced his decision to close the Cleveland facility—to reduce the corporation's involvement in truck component production, to reposition the corporation toward higher technology industries, and to free resources for alternative investments. Under the circumstances, with a restructured market place, increased competition, and reduced expectations for long-run rates of return, this particular plant stood little chance of being saved.

In retrospect, too little was done too late. Only a remarkable economic recovery with increased demand for truck components would have saved this facility. Even then it is not clear that the long-term future for the facility was very good. Only the introduction of new products at the plant would have assured its long-term viability. Such a development would have been unlikely in the face of the corporate chairman's announced policies and the continued ownership of the plant by the corporation.

Conclusions

As noted in the Introduction, one of the more popular explanations for Cleveland's loss of plants and jobs is the "poor labor climate"—high wages, restrictive work practices, and the belligerent nature of its labor-management relations.[5] The three cases reviewed in this chapter suggest that this is a simplistic explanation. Proposals to lower wages, eliminate restrictive work practices and generally improve the "labor climate" will not, by themselves, guarantee jobs.

Unfortunately, this is the message that is often conveyed, despite the fact that the matter of job security is much more complex. In all three cases reviewed here, management confirmed that wage and benefit costs were not the immediate cause of plant shutdown, that restrictive work practices had never been a problem or had recently been substantially reduced, and that the labor climate had improved. Rather, it was the change in the marketplace for products produced that led to closure.

On the other hand, the product market explanation for closure places emphasis on the near term past. Such a short-run perspective—what could or could not have been done in the last six months—is also deceptive. A longer-run view suggests that some focus on the labor climate may, indeed, be appropriate. In the first case, it is clear that the single product design for the plant and the company's reliance on that product to keep the Blue Water Seafood plant viable was a high risk strategy. In Custom Lumber Products, the limited range of uses for the mill was also a factor leading to its closure. In the third case, the continued narrowing of product lines produced in the Cleveland Truck Components plant reduced the viability of that plant. The lesson for surviving managers, employees, and unions is that pressure must continually be applied to bring new products (and new technologies) into an existing plant. To rely on any product very far into the future is unwise. The marketing concept of finite "product life cycle" should be apparent.

A second lesson is that some margin for uncertainty should always be present. It is not sufficient that a plant is breaking even or making a small profit. Employees and their unions must ask several key questions. (1) Are the profits of this plant so slim that a sudden unforeseen jolt to factor costs, such as energy prices, could lead to red ink? (2) Is this plant the high cost producer so that if a decline in product demand occurs, it will be the first plant to close? If the answer to either of these is affirmative, immediate steps should be taken to transform the plant either to produce its existing product more efficiently *or* to bring in new products that will "broaden the portfolio" or add to profitability.

These three cases illustrate better than any others included in this study that it is never too early to think about preserving plants and jobs. It is not the intention of this study to argue that any plant can be saved at any given point. Beyond some point, no rational economic action can sustain a plant. The message is to encourage early recognition of such a point—before it is reached—and to do something about it.

The next chapter illustrates cases where timely recognition did occur and plants were saved. The most likely scenario for all four cases in the next chapter is that *all* would have been closed had the parties not acted to save them.

NOTES

1. Daniel A. Littman and Myung-Hoon Lee, "Plant Closings and Worker Dislocation," *Economic Review*, Federal Reserve Bank of Cleveland (Fall 1983).

2. Robert B. McKersie and William S. McKersie, *Plant Closings: What Can Be Learned from Best Practice*, Washington, DC: Government Printing Office; and Paul Gerhart, "Finding Alternatives to Plant Closure," IRRA Spring Meeting, *Labor Law Journal* (August 1984) for a discussion of alternative strategies in the U.S. and U.K.

3. The company, industry, and several key facts in this case have been disguised to protect confidentiality.

4. The name of the company has been withheld at the request of management.

5. *Cleveland Tomorrow—A Strategy for Economic Vitality*, Cleveland Tomorrow Committee, December 1981, pp. 5-6.

3
Why Plants Are Saved

Decisions to reduce or to relocate business operations are made in a competitive world with constantly shifting relative advantages. These shifts include the level and location of demand for products; the kind and cost of transportation of raw materials—as well as finished products; the relative tax burdens; the relative costs of inputs such as raw material, labor and energy; [and] *the competitive adrenalin level in the company and the industry.*[1]

The preceding chapter has demonstrated that reduced profits and consequent plant closure can result for a variety of reasons and that the labor climate can be a contributing factor even if it is not an immediate cause.

If plants with a poor labor climate are to be saved, a substantial investment in improved labor relations is necessary. This statement can be interpreted in the psychological sense, i.e., that a strong personal commitment to the process by both union leaders and management is essential to its achievement. It can also be interpreted in a traditional economic sense, particularly for management. Both time and intellectual resources are money. Such an investment in the labor climate must be weighed against alternative uses such as closing the plant with the poor labor climate and opening a new plant elsewhere.

The four plants in this chapter share the common characteristic that all were threatened with closure, explicitly in three cases and implicitly in one, during the early 1980s, and all would probably be closed now had there been no investment to improve the labor climate. At the end of 1985, all plants were still in operation and all had higher levels of employment than at the time of negotiations.

Cleveland Twist Drill

Until 1967, this Cleveland cutting tool plant served as headquarters for an international, century-old, family-owned company. The company has been the industry innovator for new cutting tools and production methods and has an international reputation for high quality. In 1967, the company merged with another Cleveland-based machine tool company to form Acme-Cleveland. At first, the new parent corporation exercised little direct influence on the plant's philosophy and operating style.

During the 1967-1981 period, profits for both the plant and the corporation fell dramatically. The union's spokesman indicated that the Cleveland facility was still in the black, but the crucial question was whether the level of profits at the Cleveland plant was acceptable to management and influential stockholders in the corporation. Productivity in the Cleveland plant was high, but there were also relatively high hourly wage and benefit costs. An incentive/profit sharing program, originally implemented at the plant in 1914, had produced an average hourly wage rate of $12.50 with benefit costs of nearly $9.00 per hour (due in part to the high average age of the workforce). Thus the plant had hourly labor costs of nearly $22.00 an hour, versus an industry average of about $12.00.

Foreign competition was also a major element leading to lower profits. According to the union spokesman, mass production of products with somewhat lower quality had become possible through technological innovation. Customers had begun to turn to these products rather than pay the price for the high quality products produced by older technologies in the Cleveland plant. Moreover, there had been considerable pressure by foreign governments to require "off-set" production within their countries or "domestic content" for imported products. Thus foreign markets were lost.

Competition for the plant came as much from within the corporation as from external sources. Prior to 1981, the company had opened several new production facilities in North Carolina, Rhode Island and Kentucky. None was unionized and all were newer facilities than the Cleveland plant (portions of which were built in the 1880s). Although new production equipment had been developed and introduced in the Cleveland plant within the past 10 years, some of it had been moved to the plant in North Carolina. The company was in a position to move production out of Cleveland and into one of the unorganized plants without a major disruption.

In 1981, a new chief executive officer was appointed by the board. The paternalism which had been characteristic of the company in prior

years was virtually eliminated by this new CEO. He and his newly appointed subordinate at the plant began to institute immediate changes.
Major personnel cuts were made among salaried and white-collar
employees. According to the personnel director, about half of the
managerial workforce at the plant was in total shock. The other half
welcomed the changes as necessary for company survival with comments like, "It is about time." Union-management relations also changed
dramatically. The independent union, which had organized in the 1930s
with the tacit approval of the family-owners, found itself playing a completely new game.

Employment levels in the plant had reflected economic conditions
over the past 10 years, as well as the movement of production to other
plants. In 1967, employment peaked at 1300 bargaining unit employees;
after operating at lower levels throughout most of the 1970s, a peak
employment of 1050 was reached in 1979. From this point there was
a steady decline until June 1982, when employment was approximately 550. At that time, the first vote on concessions failed to carry, and
the company immediately moved about half the production out of the
Cleveland plant.

Employer Decision

The employer's position was that in order to continue producing cutting tools in the Cleveland plant, redesign of the production facility with
considerable investment would be necessary. These changes would not
be made, however, if labor costs were to remain high and if labor was
not going to be flexible with regard to retraining and reassignment. It
was in this context that a seniority grievance arose and that the employer
initiated informal discussions concerning concessions in the spring of
1982. The CEO's position was that unless substantial concessions were
made and other changes implemented in the plant, he would relocate
production to other plants where the necessary changes could be made.

Union Awareness

When the austerity programs were applied to the salaried employees,
rank-and-file union members began to sense that top management's attention would eventually turn to them as well. Most of the salaried
employee adjustments took place toward the end of 1981, so that by
early 1982, the employees in the bargaining unit were anticipating the
discussions which followed.

With the actions of the corporation in the winter of 1981-82, the strategy of the new CEO was becoming clearer. From the union spokesman's perspective, the CEO's objective was to decentralize production by installing new production equipment in other locations rather than in Cleveland so that the corporation would gain leverage to deal with the union and have an alternative if negotiations failed. Initial discussions were held with members of the union bargaining committee to tell them about problems at the plant. In April 1982, there were meetings with groups of employees on an informal basis. According to the personnel director, the bargaining committee for the union accurately communicated to the employees what it was hearing from management. In general, the committee members laid out the details factually and without distortion. Despite the reality of the cutbacks that had already been implemented at the plant, and despite the existence of the company's other facilities, neither the bargaining committee nor the employees believed that the corporation would actually close the Cleveland plant. The lack of credibility was partly due (1) to the employees' belief that they were essential and irreplaceable, (2) to their lack of familiarity with the marketplace, and (3) to the sudden change in management style and approach.

Decision Process

In late April 1982, the parties began negotiations. Although the contract still had 18 months to run, the company demanded a new 43-month contract containing wage and benefit cuts amounting to at least $4.00 an hour, according to one newspaper report. The concessions included a 31-month wage freeze, an end to the cost-of-living allowance, cuts in incentive pay, elimination of four paid holidays, reduced vacations, and replacement of a 68-year-old profit-sharing plan with a 50 percent matching savings plan for workers. According to the union president, in some cases the wage and incentive pay cuts could have reduced a worker's wages by more than $8.00 per hour. At the time these demands were made in April 1982, the union president was told that the company regarded its proposals on wages and benefits to be nonnegotiable.

Included on the management bargaining team was a new vice-president who had recently been hired away from another Cleveland company. In his previous job, he had been a key figure in a lengthy strike after which the union lost its certification. In the initial sessions with the union at the plant, this individual was quoted by the personnel director as having said, "I'm here to do a job. If I need to move the work out, I will."

This attitude and the company's rigid position alienated the union and created animosity in the first meeting. There was no movement on the part of either party.

The union finally took the company's proposals to the membership for a vote in June. Prior to the vote, the company had mailed a letter to employees stating, "If the package is rejected: (1) Our costs will be too high to make most tools in Cleveland; (2) The significant amount of money that could have been spent in Cleveland is likely to be spent elsewhere to make the company competitive." The union viewed this letter as either a threat or a bluff. In either case, the membership was inclined to "show the company" and the proposal failed 19-507.

Well after the 1982 negotiations, the union president acknowledged that the economics of the cutting tool market had actually driven those negotiations. He was aware of the market conditions, although his membership was not as well-informed. It is clear now, however, that the personal animosity that had developed during negotiations served only to exacerbate the difficult bargaining that was necessary. In retrospect, the personnel manager felt that the company pushed too fast and had too little credibility with the workforce. Despite what had happened in the salaried ranks, many of the employees simply refused to believe that the corporation could close the Cleveland plant completely. Another factor was that the union leadership and its constituency were in step with each other. Management misunderstood this unity prior to the first-round vote.

Union leaders and members were not convinced prior to the election that the corporation would close down its Cleveland operations. On the other hand, they did sense that some changes were needed and that future investment in the plant might be affected if such changes were not made. According to a newspaper report, after the first election, the union requested that the company again enter negotiations with the union concerning company needs.

Management agreed to meet but stated that the company was "disappointed with the results of the vote, and won't be investing the type of money in the facility we would have otherwise."[2] It implemented a plan to expand production elsewhere by purchasing a vacant warehouse in North Carolina in September 1982. Modifications were made in that facility, and by December 1982, first production was coming out of that plant. About half of the production capacity in the Cleveland plant was relocated to North Carolina. As a result, nearly half of the jobs in the Cleveland plant were eliminated.

What might be characterized as *stage two* of the decision process involved a seniority grievance. As a result of the company's 1981 modifications to the production process, particularly the realignment from process orientation to product line orientation in the plant, a seniority grievance had been filed by the union. It involved a conflict between departmental and plantwide seniority. The company's position was that the old seniority provision was no longer applicable or feasible because of the realignment of production in the plant. The company offered to work out alternative plans with the union, but the union forced the matter to arbitration. Although the union president was certain that he would win in arbitration, the arbitrator ultimately ruled in the company's favor with a decision that came back to the parties in August 1982.

About that time, union leaders contacted Mayor Voinovich of the City of Cleveland and asked him to look into the potential job loss associated with the company's purchase of the North Carolina warehouse. After some investigation, the mayor apparently responded to the union through his chief economic advisor that the company was indeed serious about moving out of Cleveland completely unless the union made concessions. The mayor had also been convinced that the company had a valid argument.

The mayor's message, the results of the spring negotiations, the arbitrator decision, and the plan to move equipment to the new North Carolina location convinced the union president that new discussions with the company were critical. At the same time, the personnel manager recognized that although the union had indicated a willingness to discuss the company's needs further, the union president was reluctant to push for such negotiations because such a move would signal weakness on the part of the union to the company. A mediator from the Federal Mediation and Conciliation Service office in Cleveland offered to help initiate discussions and both parties responded positively.

The second round of negotiations was conducted with a total news blackout. In the earlier negotiations, stories had appeared in the Cleveland newspapers after every negotiating session. This publicity had served to undermine the positions of both bargaining teams, but particularly that of the union team. The company negotiating team for the second round also excluded the abrasive vice-president. A more conciliatory team that included an attorney, the plant manager and the plant industrial relations manager represented the company. Finally, in light of the experience with the first vote, the company did not send letters to the homes of members or attempt any direct communication. It was clear that the union leadership could communicate accurately and effectively with the constituency and that it reflected the constituency's views. Consequently, the company had to rely on these leaders' ability to convince the constituency to vote for the concessions which were ultimately agreed upon after the second round of negotiations.

In the view of the plant personnel manager, the turning point in negotiations came subsequent to the union's filing of an unfair labor practice charge with the National Labor Relations Board about Thanksgiving 1982. Until that time, little progress had been made in negotiations. The company offered a conciliatory gesture at the time of the filing, and within two weeks the union had withdrawn the ULP charge. Subsequent to that time, a total of 15 meetings were held with the federal mediator through April 1983. Both parties agreed that the mediator was extremely effective in getting the message across to the union concerning the reality of the company's intentions. The mediator was a former union president. This gave him the credibility to persuade the union committee that concessions were absolutely critical. Union members ratified the concessions 141-86.

From the company's point of view, crucial changes in the agreement included a reduction in average labor costs for the plant. The average wage rate was reduced by $3.00 per hour with wages frozen for the duration of the contract. The cost-of-living allowance was also eliminated. Other significant factors for the company were the reduction of the number of job descriptions and labor grades and a modification of the seniority provision in the contract. The union not only accepted the new provisions in the contract, but also agreed that it would not institute any form of legal action through the NLRB or the courts with respect to the company's previous relocation or consolidation of operations.

In return for the changes in the agreement, the company agreed not to transfer the manufacture of existing product lines to any company facility except those specifically identified in the company proposal that was ratified by the union.

Contributing Factors

The change in management as well as in management style immediately prior to the company's demand for negotiations and concessions was a significant factor blocking credibility. Moreover, the style of the vice-president and his reputation concerning his previous antiunion activities (whether deserved or not) were significant factors leading to animosity in the initial round of bargaining with the union.

It could be argued that the new aggressive style of management was crucial in order to save the plant. Had the austerity programs not been implemented at that time, it is problematic whether the plant could have survived. At the same time, there is no question that the autocratic aggressive approach of some of the new management team interfered with effective communications and motivated negative union responses.

The union in this case was not particularly militant, nor had it ever had any difficulty negotiating agreements with the paternalistic-style management of the old company. One could argue that since the union members had received the best in benefits and wages, there was no reason for militancy. At the same time, however, the tradition of militancy and resistance to management initiatives did not exist in this particular case. Instead, this attitude appears to have arisen in response to the style of management which was suddenly imposed in the situation.

It is also apparent that the union leadership was both responsive to, and able to lead, its constituency. The potential for union politics to disrupt bargaining and prevent or block realistic negotiations does not seem to have been a significant problem in this case.

Negotiations and ratification were entirely within the control of the local union president and his constituency. On the management side, details of negotiations were clearly in the hands of plant management, although the CEO of the corporation had an interest in the outcome and the total cost of production in Cleveland. Local plant-level control was important in providing the flexibility and rapid turnaround in posture for both parties that was essential for saving the plant.

Final Outcome

As part of their agreement, the parties negotiated a new productivity gain-sharing incentive program to be implemented in April 1984. Although it was somewhat delayed, that program was adopted and put into effect as of September 1, 1984. The long-term prognosis for this plant is uncertain. Labor costs are still well above industry average, and the physical facilities in Cleveland are not conducive to the most efficient production configuration. In early 1985, however, the personnel manager informed researchers that one production line that had previously been moved to North Carolina had been returned to Cleveland, and that employment was up.

On September 1, 1986, *Crain's Cleveland Business* reported the company had moved its Cynthiana, Kentucky plant production to Cleveland. Under a new agreement with the union, employees who filled the "Kentucky jobs" would be paid less than the rate for other jobs in the plant. Over 100 new positions were created in Cleveland by the move.

Inferences

This case illustrates as well as any in the study the impact that changing markets have on traditional, staid bargaining relationships. Management is always first to recognize the need for change. The case also illustrates that change may be more difficult to achieve with new (unknown) management.

Credibility was a crucial issue here, as was the style of management in the negotiations. Even with hard evidence concerning wage rates and the competitive position of the plant, the union was not prepared to accept management statements concerning the potential for closing the plant. Even more compelling was the fact that substantial austerity programs had already been implemented with the termination of nearly half of the white-collar/supervisory workforce at the plant.

The purchase of the plant in North Carolina, the loss of an arbitration decision concerning seniority, the contact with the Mayor and his associates, the introduction of the Federal Mediation and Conciliation Service mediator into the situation helped overcome the credibility problem.

A key question is whether the company's purchase of the warehouse in North Carolina and its subsequent move of over half of the plant's jobs to North Carolina was necessary for the union's recognition of reality. That position is certainly arguable. On the other hand, it may be that a more tolerant and patient personal style by management during the first round of negotiations might have permitted the corporation to avoid the expense associated with this move to North Carolina.

Ohio Rubber

The similarities between Cleveland Twist Drill and Ohio Rubber are substantial. Both began as family-owned firms in what are now old facilities. Both were bought by or merged into larger companies in the recent past. The parent companies established alternative manufacturing facilities so that there was potential for a "tragedy scenario." The companies' needs for concessions to keep the plants competitive were strong enough to evoke *bona fide* closure threats at the time of negotiations. Finally, credibility played a role in the pace of negotiations and nearly led to plant closure.

A family-owned rubber company built the original part of Ohio Rubber over 100 years ago in a Cleveland suburb. The plant produces molded rubber products mainly for the auto industry—"everything that's made from rubber except the tires." In 1952, the company was purchased by a conglomerate from outside the Cleveland area. There has been essentially no change in the product mix or markets for the firm's products since the 1950s. A very large proportion of the plant's output is sold to one major auto manufacturer, and this arrangement has a substantial impact on products produced, quality control and the level of activity at the plant. If this major customer were lost, the plant would inevitably close.

Bargaining unit employment at the plant reached nearly 1000 in the middle 1970s. By late 1982, however, the number of employees had fallen to 375. Subsequent to the negotiation that saved the plant in January 1983, employment grew to slightly over 500.

The profitability of the plant is highly dependent on volume. The slump in auto sales during the 1982 recession substantially affected the performance of the plant. By late 1982, this plant was losing nearly $600,000 per month.

Despite the efforts of the company to introduce rubber industrial products that are highly specialized and engineered to meet customer specification, these new products do not account for a substantial amount of business at the plant. The corporation recently purchased another rubber products manufacturer, closed its principal manufacturing facility, and integrated some of its operations into the Cleveland plant in order to boost volume.

The source of competition that led to the plant closing threat in Cleveland was the other company locations rather than external or foreign competition. These other locations were much smaller facilities with smaller optimal operating levels. They also had lower labor costs and in two cases were nonunionized.

Employer Decision

The proximate cause of the crisis for the Cleveland plant was the 1982 recession. The corporation's policies concerning the development of smaller new plants in Pennsylvania and Indiana, as well as its purchase of another rubber products company in the early 1980s, contributed to this plant's difficulties, however. In late 1982, the company's principal production facility was the Cleveland plant, but specialized products were being produced in its smaller plants in Tennessee, Illinois, Texas, Indiana and Pennsylvania. The Texas and Indiana plants had been established during the 1970s as satellite plants for the Cleveland operation because volume was so large at that time.

In early 1982, the company's principal customer in the auto industry demanded that prices be reduced. This compounded the difficulty for the company. The customer was demanding long-term contracts from the company at progressively lower prices.

Despite the fact that the principal production plant for an acquired rubber products company had been closed in 1981 (following a long strike), there was still a need to consolidate operations to achieve economies of scale and improve the overall cost picture. The parent corporation was fully aware of the cyclical nature of the automotive rubber supply industry and has traditionally covered the Cleveland plant's losses for brief periods. The size of the plant's monthly loss, and the continuation of these losses for an extended period of time, could not be tolerated, however. Corporate management's principal concern was reducing cost. It did not prescribe the method for achieving cost reduction, but left the solution in the hands of the rubber company.

The choice facing the company was not whether to close facilities, but which of its facilities to close. Management realized that Cleveland was a desirable location to maintain because the plant there was the only completely integrated facility. Moreover, it was close to the market for its products. Finally, some of top management identified with the plant since they had begun their careers there and they felt an obligation to long-service employees at the Cleveland plant. Labor and utility costs were higher in Cleveland, however, and management could not justify the maintenance of the Cleveland facility while other lower cost production facilities were readily available to the company in its satellite locations.

One other important element was the company's need to modernize its production facilities. New technology for the production of floor mats was available to the company. By 1983, management had to make a decision on where these facilities would be located. In effect, the negotiations in late 1982 and early 1983 concerned the location of these new mat production facilities.

Union Awareness

The company had utilized news bulletins to keep its employees informed concerning conditions at the plant—both good and bad. The union had always been advised about plans for new product lines and redevelopment in the plant. As a result, according to one management spokesperson, the employees were less skeptical concerning conditions in late 1982 than they might have been in a more tightly controlled environment.

Shortly after the corporation had made it clear that it would no longer absorb the extraordinary losses of the rubber company, the vice-president in charge of labor relations approached the union president requesting that the rubber workers' union open contract negotiations early. The contract then in effect was not due to expire until January 1984. On November 4, 1982, a letter went to the union president stating that the company was going to close plants and explaining that the 1981-84 contract terms had been agreed to with the expectation that business would support them. In addition, the company asserted that it was impossible to meet the demands by the principal customer of the company for multiple year contracts with price reductions and fulfill the terms of the 1981-1984 labor contract. Finally, the letter made it clear that unless the losses of the Cleveland plant were reduced, the corporation would act to close it. The letter went on to summarize the changes in labor costs that the company wanted to implement. This letter clearly spelled out the company's objectives and needs, as well as the alternatives if these needs were not met.

The union president was convinced that the contentions in the letter were essentially true and that some sort of labor cost modification would be necessary. He was aware that the company had previously closed one of its plants in South Carolina. He was also aware that a plant owned by another company, a competitor, had been closed. His comment during one interview was that the economic conditions of the industry were "a known fact." Nonetheless, there remained some skepticism concerning the need for the degree of contract modification sought by the company. Among both the rank and file and some elected officials, there was resistance to the proposals put forth by the company to reduce labor costs.

Decision Process

On the recommendation of the president of the rubber company, a general meeting for all hourly and salaried employees was called to explain the company dilemma and what it would take to keep the plant operating. Although adjustments in salaried employee conditions were necessary, the future of the plant depended on the acceptance of contract adjustments by unionized hourly employees. A corporate executive vice-president who had formerly served as president of the Rubber Company and had been associated with the plant for many years conducted the meeting. During the early part of November, the parties met and reached a tentative agreement which would have cut fifty cents per hour from labor costs at the plant. Most of these savings were prospective. They involved no immediate cuts in wages or benefits for employees. The membership of the local, however, was not persuaded that concessions were necessary and refused to ratify the proposal.

Shortly after the membership meeting, the company determined that the proposed concession package was not nearly enough to save the plant. In fact, it had concluded that labor cost reductions for the future would have to be closer to $2.00 per hour in order to justify maintaining the Cleveland facility. The parties resumed negotiations without much optimism.

After intensive negotiations in early December, the union committee agreed to call another membership meeting for Sunday, December 12. Management submitted a complete proposal to the union committee on Friday, December 10, expecting the proposal to be discussed and possibly ratified at the union meeting Sunday. In return for concessions amounting to about $1.50 per hour, management offered to close its Tennessee plant and move its operations, and about 20 jobs, to Cleveland. Management also offered to place its new floor mat process in Cleveland and keep it there for the term of the agreement. The concessions did *not* require any employee to take a cut in current wages.

At the Friday meeting, the union brought up a matter concerning work assignment—in particular, an attempt by a supervisor to assign the task of cleaning a rest room to an employee not regularly assigned to such tasks. The union demanded assurances that no such assignments could be made in the future, and when such an assurance was not forthcoming they walked out of the meeting and cancelled the scheduled Sunday union meeting.

It was suggested by one interviewee that the real reason for the union's refusal to submit the package of company proposals to the union meeting was political. The incumbent local president had called the December 12 meeting anticipating there would be general support from the union negotiating committee for the package. When the committee decided to make no recommendations, he was fearful that he would be the sole union representative identified with concessions. In the meantime, a formal local president, who had been defeated for reelection by the incumbent, had become the informal leader of the "stop concessions" group. It was hypothesized that the only way the incumbent could get away from his exposed position was to cancel the meeting.

The response of the company president was to write a letter to all employees outlining the preceding events and offers by the company. His letter noted the cancellation of the meeting, called attention to the excuse for cancelling it, and stated the consequences that would surely follow.

> We were informed this morning, Saturday, December 11, that the Committee would not submit the proposal to the membership, and that Sunday's membership meeting was being called off.

> We were told by the Committee that they were absolutely unwilling to review the proposals *until* the Company agreed that no . . . employee whose job is done could be asked to clean a restroom—even if it is voluntary—to finish out a day's work instead of being sent home without pay . . . This issue could have easily been resolved in a normal grievance meeting, if a grievance had been filed. It had no place in such an important negotiation session except as either a pressure tactic by the Union Committee or a technique employed by the Union to avoid the real subject. We find it incomprehensible that such an issue would lead to the complete breakdown of our talks and, therefore, place all our jobs in jeopardy.

> We have tried our best and have obviously failed to convey to the Union Negotiating Committee the drastic consequences

which will result from the failure to negotiate reductions.
We obviously must now make our future plans for production elsewhere at the earliest possible date.

The company issued a press release which included the letter it circulated to its employees. On Sunday, December 12, 1982, the *Cleveland
Plain Dealer* featured a story in which it stated that the plant would
be closed and the production would be moved out of the Cleveland area.
A Cleveland TV station also presented a synopsis of the situation, in-
terviewing both company and union spokesmen.

A management spokesman stated that since the plant is not in
downtown Cleveland, but in a fringe suburb, it is seen by the community
as "its plant." Moreover, its location has allowed its workforce to live
in a concentrated group rather than be spread all over the metropolitan
area. Naturally, they are part of the community and the possibility for
interaction with other citizens in the community is great. This factor
was recognized by the company and it concluded that if the community
as a whole could be convinced of the company's problems and its sincerity concerning the closing threat, the community would be an ally in
their effort to retain the facility.

Although no hard evidence of the community's role was available,
the company was convinced that its public relations effort did have an
impact. As a result of the publicity surrounding the cancellation of the
meeting, considerable pressure was mounted in the community. Many
members informally urged the union committee to do something, and
negotiations with the company were resumed about a week later. After
negotiating from mid-December through the early part of January, the
parties had reached agreement on a number of contract modifications,
but not on all issues raised by the company. The union committee agreed
to take the agreed-upon items, and company proposals on the remaining issues, to a membership vote, but without a formal recommendation by the union committee. The membership of the local voted 178
to 125 to approve all contract modifications including company
proposals.

The new agreement provided for reduced vacations and holidays, a
modified health plan, and the elimination of a scheduled wage increase
for 1983. The company's position throughout negotiations was that if
the union could determine alternative ways to reduce labor costs that
would be politically acceptable, the company would consider them. For
management, the goal had been to reduce labor costs by $2.00 per hour,

but it was willing to allow for cost increases, subsequent to that cut, provided the volume in the Cleveland plant rose. Wage increases during the term of the new three-year agreement were provided contingent on volume in the plant.

The turning point in negotiations for the union president concerned the guarantee of new production facilities in the Cleveland plant. He wanted assurances that the company would invest in the new mat processing line in Cleveland and that it would not produce this product elsewhere during the term of the agreement. It is clear from the events described above, however, that even after these assurances, which were contained in the company president's letter of December 11, the political situation within the bargaining unit had to be resolved before the settlement could be finalized.

Contributing Factors

The different *personal styles* of key management actors at different stages in the decision process are apparent. During the first round of talks with the union in November 1982, the corporation sent the corporate vice-president of labor relations to Cleveland for negotiations. He was characterized by one spokesperson as a "young guy" who had a negative impact. Union negotiators and local union members were concerned about the capacity of such an individual to understand and empathize with their position. They felt that he was more likely to "hit and run." This individual was compared, perhaps unfairly, with a corporate negotiator who had, from the union's point of view, forced the union to the point of a strike in 1973. The employees were repelled by this company negotiator and he was unable to make any headway with the union concerning contract revisions.

Two key individuals for management stand out as having had a positive impact. Their credibility was substantial and the success of negotiations was primarily due to the role of these men. The first of these managers, the local vice-president of employee relations for the rubber company, had been with the company for 13 years in his present position. As a result, the union and employees were confident that he had as much at stake in these negotiations as they did. Another key player was an executive vice-president for the parent corporation who had long tenure in the Cleveland plant before he was promoted into the parent corporation. Even though he was no longer physically located in Cleveland, the union and the employees trusted his assertions during these negotiations.

Perhaps one of the most critical ingredients in this case was the patience and enduring energy of management negotiators to "stick with it." Others may have lost interest much earlier or would have been intolerant of union political considerations. On this dimension, Ohio Rubber contrasts sharply with Cleveland Twist Drill in its stage one negotiations.

On the union side, the president of the local had been elected to that position in October 1980, defeating the incumbent. The new president favored negotiating with the company to develop a package that would give employees the greatest assurance of job security with the least sacrifice in terms and conditions. The former president, on the other hand, opposed any renegotiation and led a sizeable minority faction within the local on this issue. His influence was perhaps the principal impediment to an early resolution of the negotiations at the plant.

It is interesting to speculate about the role of economic conditions as they might have affected the political choices of the rank and file in this case. By 1980, the industry had already begun to suffer economic reverses and employees were aware of that. There was a lengthy strike followed by the complete closure of the other major employer in the community about that time. That closure added credibility to the statements by Ohio Rubber that the Willoughby Plant could close. Though it is speculative at best, such circumstances may have had a bearing on the voters' choice of the less militant of two individuals for a key negotiating role.

Three months after the new agreement had been signed, in May 1983, there was a local union election for district delegate to the national union. This office is frequently held by the president but not necessarily so. The president won election as the district delegate over opposition from the former president, with a margin of victory greater than the 178 to 125 vote on the contract renegotiation package in January. He viewed this outcome as a vote of confidence for him and his renegotiation of the agreement.

As a postscript, by September 1984, the local union president had resigned to accept a staff position with the international union. He was replaced in office by the more militant former president. The introduction of new products at the plant coupled with a modest improvement in economic conditions may have had a bearing. The impact of this development on the future of the union-management relationship and company plans at the Cleveland plant is unclear at this point. The new president promised to win back all the previous concessions. This turn of events may have some impact on the prognosis for the plant.

Another element that helps explain the successful resolution of negotiations in this case is the *history of union-management relations.* Ohio Rubber, like Cleveland Twist Drill, has had a long history of bargaining with few major work stoppages, the last one in 1963, and low grievance rates. Only two or three grievances have reached arbitration within the past fifteen years. From July 1982 through June 1983, however, five grievances went to arbitration. These related primarily to the new incentive system installed by management. In the opinion of one union spokesman, the company vice-president of employee relations had been accused by top management at the corporation of "giving the plant away to the union." For that reason, he forced some of the grievances into arbitration in order to have the arbitrator "take him off the hook."

Union spokespeople expressed the view that interpersonal relations between the union and management at the Cleveland plant were excellent. Even with the introduction of new management people who were moved to Cleveland as a result of corporate consolidation, the relations between the union and managers have been good.

Part of the explanation for this harmony is the frequency of meetings between the union and management. Every two to three weeks a grievance meeting is held to review any matters at the second and third steps. As a result of these meetings, management and the union president regularly see each other and discuss virtually any issue that either wishes to raise during these meetings. On these occasions, management takes the opportunity to discuss problems or plans with the union so that there are virtually no surprises for the union president when moves are made on the management side.

The only reservation the union reported concerning management was the lack of involvement for employees with productivity problems in the plant. Employees have not been invited to participate in the broader issues of improving productivity. The union president feels that contributions could be made in this area.

Another element of similarity between Ohio Rubber and Cleveland Twist Drill is the degree of autonomy held by local negotiators on both sides. Corporate management imposed the requirement that local management reduce labor costs *or* move production to one of its alternative facilities. Details were left to local management. There was a substantial degree of overlap between corporate management and local management in this particular case, both formally and informally. As noted previously, the executive vice-president for the corporation was the former president of this division. His length of service and involvement in prior operations at this plant enabled him to exercise considerable influence without alienating existing management at the local level. Moreover, his involvement was not viewed as an intrusion but rather one of genuine interest and concern, since he had played a major role in the development of the plant.

Final Outcome

The agreement reached in January 1983 provided for a 36-month contract. Union members agreed to give up a scheduled 40 cent per hour wage increase under the cost-of-living plan and four cents in fringe benefits scheduled to begin in January. There was no cut in current wages, however. Employees also agreed to reduce holidays from 12 to 10 per year and to eliminate one week of vacation benefits for anyone eligible to receive more than one week. Group health insurance costs were reduced for the company through an increase in deductible amounts to be assumed by employees.

During the 36-month contract, the company agreed to wage increases based on a productivity formula and output measure. The latter was dependent on the number of pounds of rubber processed in the plant. A final contractual condition related to seniority for layoffs. The provision allowed seniority to be calculated on a departmental or divisional basis rather than plantwide for layoffs of up to two weeks. Finally, a scheduled increase in the pension contributions was deleted.

With respect to the productivity program negotiated in the agreement, there was some problem with implementation. The company has been attempting to revamp the incentive plan, but so far there has been resistance to the changes it has made. Obviously, to the extent that labor costs are affected, plant retention remains an issue.

For its part, the company agreed to three major provisions in a letter to the union dated January 3, 1983. Provided that the proposals negotiated by the company and the union were ratified, the company agreed to the following conditions:

1. The operations and the business of the company at its Tennessee plant would be moved to the Cleveland plant. Such a move was to be completed within three months of the effective date of the contract.

2. The new floor mat operation would be developed and retained 100 percent in the Cleveland plant and no such mat production would be maintained by the company at any location other than the Cleveland plant through the expiration date of the contract.

3. Benefit reductions and wage restraints effective with this agreement would be applicable to *all* employees in the Cleveland plant and not only to the hourly-rated employees.

Inferences

Management enjoyed a high level of credibility with union leadership and a substantial part of its constituency going into these negotiations. This was true with respect to both the company's threat to close as well as commitments it was willing to make provided the union could agree to modified contract terms. In the early 1980s, the company had already closed one of its nonunion facilities in the south and, following a lengthy strike, had closed a major production facility in another location in order to consolidate operations in Cleveland. In 1981, when the union agreed to broader job classifications and definitions for the involved work, the company agreed to transfer its wiper blade manufacturing operations to Cleveland, thus enhancing job opportunity locally. These operations had been moved and established in the Cleveland plant about six months before the plant-saving negotiations which are recounted here.

Union politics obviously played a critical role in the *pace* of these negotiations. In the context of most of the other cases included in this study, these politics would have caused failure and plant closure. Only the incredible *patience of management* to try "one more round" of negotiations led to success under adverse circumstances.

Management demonstrated so much patience that a cursory review of this case might lead one to conclude its threat to close was, in fact, a bluff. However, the size of the losses at the Cleveland plant and the realistic alternatives management had for the location of its mat production and other existing lines indicate that management was not bluffing.

Perhaps most important along this dimension was the experience of the local vice-president of employee relations in dealing with this local union. Management "knew" it could get the settlement with time. The critical deadline that eventually led to settlement was the scheduled

January 1983 wage increase and cost-of-living adjustment. They could not be paid and everyone knew it. As with most negotiations, deadlines are important to bring the process to conclusion.

Auto Parts[3]

The third and fourth plants in this chapter are parts of very large multinational corporations not based in Cleveland. Both plants were characterized by management personnel as among the worst in their respective corporations in terms of labor climate in the mid-1970s. They represent, perhaps, the quintessential examples of plants that have been saved by a reversal of the labor climate.

Auto Parts, which is owned by one of the "big three" auto companies, produces components which are shipped to an assembly plant by the corporation. A number of other plants owned by the corporation produce essentially similar products. The Cleveland plant, built in 1954, is neither the oldest nor the largest plant of its kind in the corporation, although it does occupy a crucial place in the production of certain parts for the company. The product mix at the plant has not changed substantially since the plant was opened. Employment levels at the plant have ranged from a high of 3500 employees in the mid-1960s to a low of about 1650 employees in 1980.

The attitude of top management in Detroit toward this particular plant is important. Unlike the first two plants in this chapter, where top management at the corporate level was positively biased due to sentimental attachment or other reasons, in this situation top management had the opposite bias. Conditions leading to these top management attitudes toward the plant remained unchanged throughout most of the 1970s. Historically, the plant was viewed by many managers in the corporation as "unmanageable." Few mid-level or upper-level managers in the corporation looked forward to an assignment at this plant.

In large measure this attitude developed out of the very negative labor climate at the plant. In the 1960s, the environment was extremely hostile. The union knew that the plant was crucial to the overall production network of the company and that a shutdown would cripple the ability of the corporation to produce its automobiles. In the words of one interviewee, the strategy of the union was to increase the number of employees in the plant by any means possible. Work rules were crafted in such a way as to maximize the use of employees in the plant. During that era, it appeared that the union's objective was to maximize the amount of nonwork time paid for by the company.

Production standards and their interpretation were a major source of the manageability problem, poor performance, and high labor costs in this plant. The standards were set on the basis of normal operations. Ordinarily, employees were permitted to cease work (and some went home) when standards were met. Other plants typically work "bell-to-bell," that is, they produce above standard on many days because they do not stop work when the standard is met.

Even more critical was the accounting method for down time. When mechanical breakdowns occurred, employees were credited for output as though the plant were operating normally. Thus there was little incentive for employee action to keep the plant running smoothly. The "phantom parts" that were never produced naturally increased the difficulty of managing the plant and added to the real per unit labor costs in the plant.

Although other corporate plants have developed work practices that undermine higher productivity, such practices were rarely written and were not uniformly enforced. For example, at the company's largest plant producing similar products, some of the practices were the same as at the Cleveland plant, but the local union became flexible on the maintenance of these practices during the late 1970s, since the need for increased production and profitability had become apparent. At the Cleveland plant, however, the rules have all been put into writing so that the local agreement is nearly as thick as the master agreement between the international union and the corporation. Moreover, the local has never made any concessions to improve the picture for management and has never felt that the members had any direct stake in improving the performance of the plant.

With respect to investment and technological change, the union at this plant fought the introduction of both radio-controlled cranes and automated material-handling transport. Although the union's concern for job security is understandable, these investments were crucial to keeping the plant competitive with other corporation plants. Only after 1980 did some portion of the union's leadership come to realize that if these and similar investments were not made and accepted by the existing workforce, all of the members would be out of work.

The management spokesman made one further important point concerning investment in this particular plant. He indicated that although the company had undertaken investment in new production lines, these lines are "portable." Even the large automated manufacturing systems can be disassembled and moved to other locations if the company decides to close this plant. Hence, although new investments are crucial and indicative of long-term job security, they do not necessarily guarantee the long-term existence of a particular plant.

In addition to the rules and restrictions on technological innovation that had reduced plant performance, the labor relations climate at the plant was poor. A management spokesperson quoted some statistics to substantiate the existence of such a climate. In 1965, when the plant had approximately 3500 employees, there were 6700 disciplinary actions. In addition, 200-300 grievances were filed each month. Industrial relations was so chaotic that it simply could not be managed. For its part, management was guilty of playing the same kind of game the union did. Managerial decisions would not be made on the basis of optimal operating procedures or efficient operations, but on the basis of gaining leverage for the upcoming round of negotiations. Environmental improvements would be deferred until negotiations occurred, for example. Union grievances concerning these items could then be traded off against other kinds of demands by the union.

Moreover, the plant has been among the last to settle its local negotiations in each round of bargaining with the corporation. During the 1980 negotiations, this plant was last, but it was during these negotiations that the relationship between the parties began to turn around.

A management spokesperson pointed to poor relations at the *personal* level as a capstone element that characterized managerial views of the plant. In most plants, an underlying union/employee interest has usually motivated union leadership behavior. Attacks on management have been made, but they have come out of a concern for protecting the union's interests. In this plant, that motivation has had a tendency to be lost among the personal attacks intended to destroy individuals. For this reason, the interpersonal relationships at the plant during the 1960s and 1970s were extremely poor. This perception by corporate management, many of whom had actually worked in the plant, was a major factor in targeting the plant for closure.

In summary, this plant was distinguished by its poor operational performance and poor labor-management relations prior to 1980. Throughout the company, agreements had been changed to provide for greater latitude and flexibility on the part of management so that it could respond to the "new economic climate" of the auto industry as it developed through the late 1970s and early 1980s. In other locations, where less emphasis has been placed on written work rules and "working by the book," this movement has been difficult, but not impossible to implement. In the Cleveland plant, however, lack of interpersonal trust and the historical reliance on tight language created a condition in which the members of the union and management felt uncomfortable with flexibility.

Employer Decision

In the environment of the 1979 national negotiations, the corporation had flexibility because of excess capacity. Consolidation, work transfer, and plant closure were clearly possible. In late 1979, the corporation undertook a study of the Cleveland plant in comparison with other plants in the same product division. A company spokesperson, who was a member of the study team, is convinced that the company was not bluffing when it threatened to close the plant unless local agreement modifications were made.

The plant's performance and costs were so far out of line with those of other plants producing the same product that there was no justification for keeping this facility open, particularly in light of the excess capacity of other plants. In short, performance to budget expectations, quality, and the labor relations "climate" at the Cleveland plant led to such a poor corporate perception of this plant that its future was clearly in question. Although a specific decision to close the plant had not been made at the time of the 1979-80 negotiations, this option was being considered.

Union Awareness/Decision Process

Three factors are useful to understanding the success of negotiations in this case: (1) the way the union became aware of the potential plant closing, in particular the local president's sensitivity to his plant's situation; (2) the reason for the corporation's credibility—namely, the local president's careful investigation of the facts, both at the local level and with the assistance of the international union; and (3) the local president's ability to present the case to the local membership and obtain their ratification of the changes. The way the union became aware of the potential closure and the decision process by which the plant was ultimately saved are so intertwined that a discreet discussion of these two elements is not possible in this case.

Substantive negotiations with the company were limited. The company advised the union that if its "bare bones" offer concerning changes in local working conditions were not adopted, it intended to close the facility. During the course of the local union's investigation, its contacts with the corporation in Detroit and its communications with the international union, the local president recognized that the demands made by the company were no more onerous than those placed upon, and accepted by, other local unions producing the same products elsewhere. Therefore, it is not the negotiations process between the company and union which deserves special attention here, but the three crucial elements noted above.

In 1979, master contract negotiations led to a new nationwide contract between the corporation and the national union. In July of that year the parties at the Cleveland plant commenced negotiations for a new local supplemental agreement. The company attempted to modify certain terms of the agreement, but little headway had been made by early 1980. The local president had been in office for less than a year at that point when a rumor reached him that an entire production line representing a substantial portion of the bargaining unit was going to be moved to another corporate location. There were several other rumors relating to smaller moves to different locations. He decided that investigation of these rumors would be appropriate.

He met with the national director of the union responsible for corporate level labor-management relations. The national director agreed to set up a meeting in Detroit between the local president and selected corporate officials including the corporate vice-president for manufacturing. The corporate vice-president bluntly indicated that this particular local union had been more militant than others in the company over the years and that the company had made a larger number of concessions on various work rules at the Cleveland plant that caused it to be relatively inefficient compared with similar plants in the corporation. He stated that unless the work rules were modified and brought into line with conditions at other plants, the Cleveland plant would be closed. Finally, he agreed to provide a list of proposals the company needed to keep the plant open. The international union was also able to supply information concerning work rules, practices, and excess capacity in other plants. The local president was aware that the plant had been allowed to deteriorate physically to a point where he thought that the company might not keep the plant open in any event. He was absolutely certain that there was no bluff involved in this case.

Subsequently, the local president met with his bargaining committee in Cleveland. He laid before the committee all the results of his investigations and conversations. At this time he encountered substantial resistance from the other members of the committee. They simply did not want to raise the issue of concessions on work rules with the membership. They understood the facts, but they would not believe the company's threat to close the Cleveland plant. Their inclination was to "stonewall" the company on its proposed work rule changes. The local president was the only member of the bargaining committee who supported a ratification of the company's position.

About this time, the corporate vice-president for manufacturing came to Cleveland at the invitation of local plant management. He attended one of the local negotiating sessions and reiterated his position concerning the needs of the company and its intentions. At that point he was challenged by the international union representative present at the meeting to put his statements ("threats") into writing. Very shortly thereafter, a letter outlining the company's needs was presented to the union by the local industrial relations manager. The letter also stated:

> . . . unless there is agreement to such changes and ratification by union members, the company will begin phasing out plant operations. It is anticipated that the phasing out would be concluded by the end of 1980.

The international representative confirmed to a project interviewer that this was a new twist for the company in negotiations. There had been frequent offhand comments about closing facilities in the past, but never before had company officials taken such a strong position and been willing to put it in writing. Moreover, the representative confirmed that the international union was able to determine output levels and capacity for other plants producing the same product. It was clear to the international that the company had more than enough capacity in other plants to absorb completely all that was being produced in the Cleveland plant.

On the other hand, not all employees at the plant were convinced, even at that point. One dissident suggested that the concession agreement was pushed by the local president solely because the skilled trades group wanted new product runs assigned to the Cleveland plant and the trades knew they would not be assigned to Cleveland until an agreement was in place. In the dissident's view, management was using the Cleveland plant as an experiment to see what it could get. According to the dissident, even though the capacity of the corporation was sufficient to cover the output produced by the Cleveland plant at the time of negotiations, the company would have had to reopen the plant at some later point in time anyway. Another dissident subsequently published a newsletter in which he characterized the local president as "the concession king."

Despite the opposition from his bargaining committee, the president of the local decided to call a general membership meeting to discuss the company's proposals. Historically, the bargaining unit had been led by the bargaining committee and had adopted bargaining committee recommendations on negotiations. With a split committee, however, the membership would be forced to make a decision. At the meeting no vote was taken. The purpose of the meeting was to present information, to allow all members to express their views, and to permit the members to ask questions. The local president advised the members to take the matter home, talk about it with their families, and decide what they would do in a vote to be cast three days later. He argued that if the plant were closed, members who were 40-45 years of age or older would simply be unable to get decent jobs of any kind, given the state of the labor market in 1980 in Cleveland. His attitude toward the younger militants in the union was "we got all this stuff, so its ours to give back." He invited them to negotiate their own contracts after all the old timers had retired.

The president's view was that the "ball game" (i.e., the economic climate) was quite a bit different in 1980 than it was in the 1960s. The president explained: "We used to kick the company's ass to get what we wanted. Now it's the other way around. . . . If you give them a hassle, they'll take their game somewhere else."

The result of the election was an 88 percent vote to accept the changes proposed by the company.

Contributing Factors

Management at the Cleveland plant over the past 25 years clearly contributed to the poor labor-management relationship and low level of plant performance. High turnover has been a major factor. Managers assigned to this plant viewed their jobs as temporary, never permanent. Often, in order to encourage people to accept assignments to the Cleveland plant, corporate managers promised them early transfers out if they would simply agree to take the job for a few years. Self-preservation or survival were a manager's principal goals; the plant's performance was secondary. Over the years, there have been individuals who have come into the plant with expectations about changing things. Universally, however, these people have been lucky to escape with their scalps, according to one interviewee.

In 1980 the plant had a new plant manager who was "up from the ranks." A charismatic and believable leader, he had a friendly rapport with everyone in the plant from top management to line worker. This manager's appointment at the time when the company's bargaining power, due to economic circumstances, was greatest, clearly worked in favor of the adoption of management's position by the bargaining unit.

Perhaps a more important consideration was the commitment of the local union president. He had a broad understanding of the environment facing the auto producers in the United States today and realized that the competitive environment was different from what it had been in the 1950s or 1960s. He was part of a tour group to visit Japanese automobile plants and had an appreciation for the kind of competition the company faced. In his speech to the membership before the ratification vote, he pointed out that certain other unions had not been flexible and that the results could be seen. In particular, he was alluding to the rubber and steel industries.

The local president was characterized by one interviewee as "not particularly impressive to meet" and certainly "not the world's greatest orator." On the other hand, he was viewed by both management and the bargaining unit members as sincere, honest, and hard-working. In part, his credibility arose from the fact that he had been a bargaining unit member and active in the union leadership at the plant almost since its inception in 1954. At one time, he was as militant as anyone else in the plant, but his long-term attachment to the plant gave him a stake in the continued operation of it. He did not want to preside over its demise.

His popularity is illustrated by the fact that after the vote to accept the management proposals in 1980, he was twice re-elected to the office of local president. Moreover, when the regional director's position was vacant several years ago, his local supported him for that position.

One explanation for the instability of labor-management relations and militancy of union leadership at the Cleveland plant is the way in which union officers are elected. There is an election in the local union every year to fill various positions. Although there is not a complete turnover of officers each year, there is always a slate of candidates with endorsements and, as a result, in the words of one spokesman, "there is nearly always a pot boiling somewhere." Part of the reason for the current stability at the Cleveland plant has to do with the long-term incumbency of the present local president. There was a consensus among individuals interviewed that although the local president had some opposition in the local, it was neither significant nor cohesive. One interviewee said that the dissidents, who are still around, "are people who can't see reality when it is looking them squarely in the face." His view was that they tend to lack the respect of the vast majority of the bargaining unit and, therefore, are of little consequence.

Undoubtedly, had the economic climate been less bleak, ratification of the agreement would not likely have occurred, regardless of who was plant manager or local president. On the other hand, without the style of leadership present on both sides, even the economic realities facing this plant would not have moved the rank and file to ratify the changes that were made in the work rules. In short, both the economic environment *and* the leadership style were necessary components to save this plant.

Another element that contributed to successful negotiations in this case was the international union. Both the international representative and higher level officials in the union provided information and contacts for the local president that were helpful to his obtaining the "facts" for decisionmaking by the local. Without this support, it is doubtful that the local union membership, or even the local president himself would have been convinced that the company was not bluffing. It is important to note, however, that the international never endorsed any position in the local referendum on the new local conditions agreement.

The key issues that caused the Cleveland plant to be at the bottom of the company's productivity/performance measure, and to be perceived by top management as the "worst" plant in the company with regard to labor-management relations, were clearly under the control of local negotiators. Hence, there was an opportunity for local individuals to have an impact on saving their plant.

Final Outcome

The most important rules modifications in the 1980 agreement related to: (1) reduction of wash-up time, (2) permission for crew leaders to work with tools under limited circumstances, (3) expansion of duties for certain occupational titles, (4) elimination of the requirement that millwrights accompany the movement of maintenance parts, (5) permission of maintenance tradesmen to drive fork-lift trucks as "tools of their trade," and (6) modification of the way production standards were applied in the plant. The production standards element contained thirteen paragraphs which substantially tightened the application of standards and, most important, the agreement eliminated "phantom production."

The union president indicated that the company had showed good faith as a result of the approval of the agreement. As soon as the contract was ratified, the company moved work back into the plant that had been contracted out or that had been moved to other locations in the company. There was a commitment from the top of the corporation to abide by the agreement even though there had been no written commitment on the part of the company to make any changes following the approval of the local agreement.

Other significant developments in the plant involve the use of an employee participation team concept that has been very effective. Although it is far from a permanent feature in the plant, according to one management spokesman, this concept has considerable support from both labor and management. The teamwork has improved communications and commitment on the part of the workforce substantially. A related effect of this settlement has been the reduction in grievance activities and disciplinary actions. As compared with the earlier time period, there have been fewer than 100 disciplinary actions taken in the past year and most of these were for absenteeism. Only about 300 grievances had been filed for the entire bargaining unit in the past year. In other words, compared with the earlier era in plant history, disciplinary actions and grievances are down by approximately 90 percent.

Inferences

The local union president's initiative to investigate what he had perceived and the rumors he had heard was the most important element in this case. The assistance and cooperation of the international union in this investigation was essential. If there had been no groundwork by the local president, the industrial relations climate in the plant (the lack of trust and traditional militancy) coupled with a vocal group of dissidents would undoubtedly have led the union to reject the agreement modifications proposed by management.

There is no way to be sure the company was not bluffing in its threat to close the plant. Management's willingness to put such a threat in writing for the first time, the fact that other corporation plants had been closed, and the general attitude of top management toward this plant based on its performance and labor climate relative to other plants in its division, all suggest that there was no bluff. Moreover, the local president and the international representative, both experienced negotiators, were convinced the company threat was genuine.

By bringing local practices into line with those at other plants, the parties gave the Cleveland plant at least an even chance for survival. The implementation of the worker participation plan and a commitment to controlling labor costs suggests that the long-run prognosis for this plant is positive.

Wrapping Materials[4]

The plant was built in the early 1950s and was acquired by a large chemical company in 1956 to produce a variety of flexible packaging materials. The present owner, a manufacturer based outside Ohio, purchased the plant in 1974 and has continued to produce much the same product for distribution to food, pharmaceutical and photographic material producers. Throughout the period from 1960 to 1975, employment varied slightly with the business cycle but remained at approximately 400 employees. After the conclusion of an 89-day strike in 1977-78, 120 people were laid off "permanently." Further cutbacks resulted in a total hourly workforce of about 170 in 1982.

Employer Decision

From the time of the 89-day strike, the corporation made no plans to introduce new products or technology into the plant. By 1981, corporate investment allocation decisions had been announced to upgrade and modernize corporate facilities nationwide, but nothing had been designated for the Cleveland plant. The plant manager concluded that the "handwriting was on the wall" for the Cleveland plant. Competing products and new technologies for producing his plant's products were beginning to erode sales and profit margins. With no new investment, the plant could not survive. Although he had been given no timetable by the corporation, he inferred that the plant would last only a few more years.

The 1981 investment decisions had been announced at the annual employee meeting in the company cafeteria. It was at that time that the plant manager first became aware of them. Most of the corporate investments were targeted for specific locations in existing plants. A few projects had been identified, but their location had not yet been fixed. Among the investments that had not yet been placed was a $6 million laminate extruder line which was to produce, for example, plastic toothpaste tubes.

The plant manager was committed to the Cleveland plant and the Cleveland area, so he decided to go after one of these new product lines for his plant. He recognized, however, that because of the image of the Cleveland plant at corporate headquarters (due in part to the 89-day strike), his goal would be difficult to achieve. Although only 20 to 30 new employees would be utilized in the new process, the manager realized that a $6 million investment in the Cleveland plant would reflect an attitude change concerning the plant at corporate headquarters and help to secure its future.

Union Awareness

In early 1982, the plant manager approached the union president to discuss the situation and a solution. It is noteworthy that the plant manager went to the union president's office on the plant floor, although the two had previously had a somewhat less than amicable relationship. The union president reported that at this long meeting there was a complete airing of many of the problems that had been brought to light as a result of the 1977-78 strike and subsequent developments at the plant.

The union president found the plant manager entirely credible with regard to the future of the plant. Furthermore, the president admitted that he and other members of the bargaining unit knew that the future of the plant was at stake. He was aware that a "sister plant" in Pennsylvania had been closed. It was clear that the corporation was consolidating into its more profitable areas. Moreover, the union leader knew that corporate management had identified the local union at the plant as "too militant."

The plant manager indicated to the local union president that new products had to be brought into the plant because much of the existing product mix and production technology was slowly becoming obsolete. Without new products the plant was doomed. The two discussed the corporate investment plans that had been laid out at the employee meeting, including the new extruder product line to be built by the company in one of several alternative locations. It was implicit that corporate planners had eliminated Cleveland as a possible extruder site because of the militant union situation, although Cleveland had numerous other advantages in the competition for the new product line such as potential governmental support and a skilled workforce.

Decision Process

The local union president called his international union. Both the international representative and his boss, the district director, became involved. It was soon apparent to the latter that although contractual concessions would be necessary to gain the new extruder line, cooperation from local public officials could also help with the infusion of public subsidies. Mayor Voinovich of Cleveland and Cuyahoga County commissioners were called upon for assistance. An Urban Development Action Grant of $600,000 was made available and industrial revenue bonds were issued by the county. The mayor also interceded with top corporate officials by inviting them to Cleveland for a meeting around the issue.

In the meantime, frequent union-management meetings were held to discuss contract revisions. Attendance expanded to include all local union officers as well as corporate employee relations representatives. A major problem for management concerned layoffs that caused certain senior individuals who were not adequately qualified to operate equipment to "bump into" such equipment when employment declined. This was an existing problem, and one that would grow worse, in management's opinion, if the new extruder process were introduced. Serious difficulties in quality control and output had already been experienced; these conditions were expected to deteriorate further.

Management's original proposal called for departmental seniority to replace plantwide seniority. The parties eventually agreed to limit bumping on certain equipment to individuals who had *bona fide* qualifications to run the job. A number of existing positions were identified, along with the key positions in the proposed new extrusion line.

The 1982 agreement to modify the seniority provision was made operable for a period of only one year, except for the proposed new extruding department. The cover letter to the proposal stated that "the changes will apply permanently to the extruding department contingent on the new extruder line coming to the Cleveland plant." In other words, the union made its concession on work rules contingent on the additional investment in the plant. Moreover, there was a tacit understanding that the new seniority provisions would be permanent after the one-year period, provided the extruding equipment actually came into existence.

After the supplemental agreement on seniority had been concluded, the parties pursued other areas in which the company had problems, particularly the large number of wage classifications and the overtime rules. In 1983, the collective bargaining agreement was extended and the modifications on these issues were incorporated.

Contributing Factors

Both the union and management spokesmen acknowledged that certain external elements were involved in the corporate decision to locate the new extrusion process in Cleveland. Many public officials, including the mayor and City Council, county commissioners, members of Congress, state representatives, and the Cleveland Growth Association played a role. In addition to the jobs created, it was important to demonstrate that a concerted effort to save jobs for Cleveland could be mounted. Success was essential for more than the employees of the plant. It was viewed as a key indicator of the future for manufacturing in Cleveland.

The plant manager and plant employee relations manager were key figures in this case. The plant manager came to the plant shortly after it had been purchased by the corporation and was committed to its continued operation. Both management and union spokespeople credited his "generalship" as the key element in saving the plant. The plant employee relations manager had been employed in the plant since shortly after it was constructed in the 1950s. He was at one time a member of the bargaining unit and the president of the local union. According to him, the labor-management relationship under the previous owner was very poor. There had been several wildcat strikes, apparently not without some provocation. ''The relationship took the plant right down the drain.'' He stated that for 17 years while the plant was under the previous owner, it was rarely profitable.

The plant manager and union president agreed in their assessment of the plant's previous owner and the impact of management attitudes on labor-management relations. The local president's view was that although the former owners had a contract, they did not abide by it. In his words, their attitude was, ''We'll violate the contract anytime we please and you can grieve if you like.'' The president indicated that as a shop steward he had personally filed over 927 written grievances in a four-year period. This number does not include other grievances which were settled verbally.

The change in ownership brought in a whole new management philosophy, however. For the most part, the local president feels that under present ownership, management attempts to abide by the agreement and to be fair with the workforce. The union has responded slowly to the change in management. In 1983, only 12 written grievances were filed in the local. The president defended the pre-1974 militancy of the union on the grounds that the previous owner's policies had mandated such a response.

The president identified paid leave for union officials as the crucial issue in the 1977-78 negotiations. Under the previous owner's last contract, a total of six union committeemen and officers had been permitted to be full-time paid union representatives. After purchasing the plant, the new owner declared that it would not accept this arrangement. Although it honored the existing agreement and promised that it would continue to do so until the terms of office expired for the existing union officers, the new owner demanded that the clause for paid union leave be removed from the contract.

Following ratification of the contract in 1978, a new election for union officers was scheduled. The bargaining unit gradually became aware of what had held up the settlement so long and reacted accordingly. The present president had not been a part of the bargaining team. He ran with a completely new slate of union officers. This group was swept into office and has retained office since the 1978 election. Most of these leaders have been unopposed in more recent elections.

Most important, local plant management saw the union election as a mandate to the leaders to stop their militant ways. In retrospect, management sees the 1977-78 strike as having at least one good element—it opened the eyes of both union members and management as to what would be necessary to save the plant. The parties finally began to talk to each other. The salaried people who came in during the strike to run the equipment began to appreciate the hourly workers' contribution and hourly workers developed a willingness to talk to management. The wall separating labor and management began to crumble.

Final Outcome

A *Cleveland Plain Dealer* editor characterized the events at the plant as the "miracle on Dobeckmun Ave."[5] (The plant is located on Dobeckmun Avenue in Cleveland.) The vice-president and general manager of the corporate division that owns the plant stated that, "the turnaround of the last two and one-half years has been nothing short of incredible and perhaps even miraculous." The mayor stated that the "project is probably Cleveland's very best example of a successful partnership of all levels of government, private business, and labor working toward the same goals—jobs and a strong position in the market place."

With the labor agreement adjustments, none of which involved pay cuts for existing workers, the obvious new industrial relations climate at the plant, and the tangible public support, corporate decisionmakers agreed to locate the new laminate extruder in Cleveland. The decision produced 68 jobs with the promise of more and the retention of existing workers.

This case has one unique feature that distinguishes it from the previous three in this chapter and ties it more closely to chapter 4. That is timing. As the *Plain Dealer* reporter stated, "Rather than play catch-up after a closing was announced, government, labor and business officials did something immediately when trouble was sensed."

A key element was the initiative of the plant manager in discussing the plant with his local union president. A candid manager who was willing to take some risk, a politically secure local union leadership, and support from the international union with respect to local union issues and the larger external political environment were ingredients for success.

Perhaps most important was the availability of corporate capital and plans for the development of a new product line *somewhere*. No matter how amicable the relationship might have grown to be at the Cleveland plant, a corporate decision to invest in an extruder line was indispensable. The existing plant was conducive to the new product line, the line had to go somewhere, so the successful set of events in Cleveland was, in part, due to a happy coincidence as well as to a significant effort on the part of the parties.

Summary

External forces—macroeconomic conditions, economic conditions specific to the industry, foreign competition, and technological change— were the drivers in each of the cases discussed in this chapter. It is easy to lose sight of these larger forces when specific cases are examined. They affect the extent to which change is necessary and the pace with which it must be implemented. They can be insidious because, for a time, they may yield a favorable environment for a plant to which both labor and management grow accustomed. When conditions suddenly change, it is often difficult for managers and especially employees to accept. This chapter has illustrated several cases where acceptance and response have occurred. Explaining these phenomena requires an institutional examination of what has occurred.

Credibility

Recognition of a plant's plight, and especially the acceptance by the union of what management is saying about it, are the crucial first steps in saving it. Several factors seem to influence credibility.

The longer the term of the relationship between the principal actors, the greater their credibility. This observation is reasonable, but several other observations were surprising. Whether or not the parent corporation is in the local area seems irrelevant to the credibility dimension. Moreover, the degree of historical militancy between the parties is not important. These conclusions are best illustrated by a comparison of Cleveland Twist Drill, with a local parent, where credibility was very slow to develop (despite the presence of other factors discussed below), with Ohio Rubber and Wrapping Materials, both of which had distant corporate parents, where credibility, at least at the union leadership level, was not a major problem.

A corollary of the conclusion that a long-term relationship is helpful is the finding that management must make its position clear by different means from those used in the past. Only a long-term relationship allows such a comparison. In Auto Parts, the willingness of corporate executives to put their threat to close the Cleveland plant in writing convinced the international representative that there was no bluff. In other cases, more extensive (verifiable) data were provided to the union than had ever been made available before. In every case, there was "something different" about management's presentation of itself and its position as compared with the way the same managers had behaved in the past.

Several elements are necessary, but not sufficient, conditions to achieve credibility. "Equality of sacrifice" is a phrase that has achieved recent popularity. To convince the rank and file that contract modifications are necessary, they must see that management is also suffering cuts in manpower or wages and benefits. Closure of other plants is also clear evidence of corporate sincerity concerning the closure threat. The reality of a nearby plant closure also affected the rank and file at Ohio Rubber, helping them to realize that even the strongest plants are not invincible. "Seeing" is not quite "believing," but it helps. Although the layoff of nearly half the white-collar workforce did not, itself, convince the workers at Cleveland Twist Drill that the plant might be closed, it is doubtful the negotiations to save the plant could have been successful without the layoff.

Another element that seems to be a part of most successful negotiations is the presentation of substantial data to employees. Not only plant profitability, but also comparisons of wages, benefits and work rules with other plants or competitors were discussed in an open meeting in most cases. Again, such sharing seems to be a necessary but not sufficient condition to save a plant. Truck Components (from chapter 2) provided the most extensive sharing of data, but the plant closed anyway. In fairness, negotiations *were successful* in the sense that the union agreed with management's demands, but economic conditions simply overwhelmed that plant.

A final factor that seems especially helpful is a history of demonstrated good faith in negotiations. At Ohio Rubber, the company moved production of wiper blades to Cleveland after modifications in the agreement were agreed upon. Even though it was not required by the agreement, the company brought a production line back to Auto Parts that had been taken elsewhere sometime prior to the agreement. The local president pointed to that as evidence of good faith and a significant factor for future negotiations.

Responses

Conclusions regarding appropriate union response and strategy in plant closing negotiations will be addressed in the final chapter. Here the discussion is limited to a few observations.

In several cases, e.g., Ohio Rubber and Wrapping Materials, concern for plant and job security led the union, with some prompting by management, to negotiate for new production lines and jobs and the introduction of new technology at the plant. Agreements in this area tended to be informal and not part of the collective bargaining agreement. A letter guaranteeing investment in return for work rule changes was provided at Wrapping Materials. At Ohio Rubber, Auto Parts, and Wrapping Materials, union spokespeople agreed that such concessions by management did more for job security than any contractual terms regarding severance pay or the perpetuation of narrow job descriptions. They were also helpful in persuading the leadership, if not the rank and file, to agree to the contractual modification being requested by the company.

Union Politics

To understand why plant closing negotiations can fail, even in the face of undeniable economic facts, one must appreciate the union as a democratic political institution. The willingness and ability of local or international leaders to try to convince the rank and file to accept contract modifications was an important element in all four cases in this chapter. It is also clear that plants would not have been saved had such leadership been absent. At Cleveland Twist Drill and Wrapping Materials there was no political opponent waiting to take advantage of the situation. At Ohio Rubber and Auto Parts, there were opponents, but the leaders in office were able to prevail. Had they been absent, the opportunists would have filled the void, thus eliminating any chance for a successful negotiation of contract changes.

As any experienced management representative knows, stable union politics are a *sine qua non* for successful negotiations. The ability of the union to act as a unified institution led by informed officers is a necessary condition for saving plants and jobs.

NOTES

1. Audrey Freedman, "Plant Closed—No Jobs," *Industrial Management* (May-June 1981), p. 13, emphasis added.

2. *Cleveland Plain Dealer*, June 18, 1982.

3. At the request of union and management spokespeople, the name and location of this plant have been withheld.

4. At the request of union and management spokespeople, the name of this plant and company have been withheld.

5. *Cleveland Plain Dealer*, April 21, 1984.

4
Securing the Future

It is clear that saving plants and jobs is dependent on securing new product lines and production processes for an existing plant, as happened at Ohio Rubber and Wrapping Materials. Sometimes the technological change is so significant, or the scale of change is so great, that expansion at the existing site is simply not practical. In such circumstances, the company faces a decision on where, not whether, to locate new facilities.

In the terms of chapter 1, the company and union are in the middle act of the tragedy scenario in such cases. If the new facility is located well away from the existing facility, it may lead not just to the closure of the existing facility, but lost opportunity for saving jobs as well. A nearby location, however, enhances the prospect for an orderly transition with no job loss.

One of the reasons an employer would consider an altogether new location is to avoid dealing with an existing union. A new local site is much more likely to be organized by the same local union than a more distant one. The strength of the employer's desire to avoid the existing union is naturally related to anticipated labor costs for the new plant and the quality of the labor climate. Negotiations that enhance the labor climate and moderate anticipated labor costs in the new plant are therefore in the interests of an existing union if one of its goals is to enhance job security for its members. In this study, we encountered two cases that illustrate such negotiations. Neither was simple and without acrimony. In both, the company did not achieve all it sought.

It is important to distinguish these cases from those where an explicit threat to close has been made. From the viewpoint of both parties, there does not appear to be as much at stake. It is difficult for employees, facing no imminent threat of job loss, to understand why they should make any concessions at all. The *quid pro quo* is difficult for them to evaluate. Then too, the contractual modifications requested by management may have very little effect on employees who remain in the old facility. Again, the long-term implications are difficult to evaluate. In short, negotiations under these circumstances are likely to be different, though not necessarily any less difficult, from those in a plant closing situation.

Air Spring[1]

Prior to 1981, the corporation in this case designed and manufactured prototype air springs for the auto industry, to replace the traditional steel coil spring, in a small area of an existing plant. Because demand for its air spring was going to exceed its production capacity in the prototype manufacturing facility, the company decided to build a new "greenfield" plant for the production of air springs. The corporation, which is based in Northeast Ohio but has worldwide production facilities, was actively considering several possible sites. One of these was in a small town in the same county as its headquarters, its prototype plant, and other production facilities. The fact that the location was within the county was significant because the local union claimed that a clause in the existing labor agreement required that all production facilities within the county, existing or developed during the term of the agreement, would be covered by its agreement. (The fact that the company disagreed is not material because the union's claim alone would create a controversy in the event the plant were located locally.) Moreover, the collective bargaining agreement allowed for seniority and bumping rights for bargaining unit members across plants throughout the local.

A site in Nebraska was also being considered by the corporation. The corporation expected that operations at either site would be unionized, but a Nebraska facility would not have been subject to the existing master or local labor agreements. The president of the local union was aware that some members of management viewed Nebraska as a more desirable site. He also knew that the corporation had closed plants in the past decade due to high labor costs, among other reasons.

Employer Decision

The corporation had some financial stake, as well as a moral commitment, in the community in which it was located. Local relocation of a facility that would eventually employ up to 350 workers as demand grew would clearly send a positive signal throughout the community. Corporate planners believed, however, that the wage and working conditions targeted as critical to the success of the air springs operations would not be accepted by union leaders and workers in the community. The local union had not made any wage or fringe concessions to the company since 1947. Although the corporation executives expected the Nebraska site would be unionized, its work rules, overtime rules and bumping process would compare favorably with similar rules in plants organized in Ohio.

Union Awareness

The local union was the bargaining representative for many nonexempt employees in corporate headquarters. The local's offices were directly across the street from the corporate offices and, as a result of this proximity, local officers and members had greater access to rumors and other "inside information" than might have been true at more distant locations.

In late 1980, the local president first learned of the corporation's intentions to build a new Air Spring plant through an off-hand remark by a management official during a meeting on a completely unrelated matter. The manager suggested that the local president "check out" a rumor he had heard that a new Air Spring plant was about to be built in Nebraska.

The local president as well as international union representatives had watched the decline of jobs in their industry in Northeast Ohio for over a decade. They perceived the building of a new Air Spring plant outside the area as a "loss" even though very few jobs would be lost immediately. For that reason, the local president called the corporate chairman about the situation. In a meeting with the chairman, union representatives were advised that the company did intend to build the plant in Nebraska, but that no firm commitments had been made. He was also informed that a site in the area was a possibility, but that given the labor agreement, the corporation could not seriously consider it. The union president urged the chairman to make no assumptions regarding the union's position on needed contract modifications. The chairman assured him that there would be more discussions with the union before a final decision was made, but he continued to be pessimistic.

Almost simultaneously, another issue of major importance arose concerning the National Master Agreement and all the locals governed by it. For many years, the Master Agreement provided *per se* double time for Sunday work regardless of total hours worked during the week. At one of its plants in a different state, the company and a different local negotiated a modification to this Sunday overtime rule applicable to that local only. The terms of the Master Agreement allowed such local modifications, provided a majority of all the locals covered by the Master approved it.

Although the local president had already cast his vote on the issue, he reminded corporate representatives of his role in that vote. In his opinion, his vote reflected his flexibility and enabled him to win corporate commitment to enter negotiations concerning the new plant shortly thereafter. Although no guarantees were made by the chairman, the impetus toward a local site, and away from the Nebraska site, had clearly been achieved. The corporation became committed to the local site provided labor cost projections were brought within the range it needed to operate the new facility profitably.

Decision Process

The local president was not operating in a vacuum. Before he could reopen negotiations, it was necessary to secure local membership approval. The first step was to obtain the support of his executive board, to which he related the entire sequence of events. The board passed a resolution of support and called a special membership meeting on the issue. Although there was some opposition, the board's resolution won support from the members. The local president then selected a special negotiating committee comprised of individuals knowledgeable about the Air Spring operations, because most issues were related to work rules. At that point, the parties were ready to meet formally for the first time.

At the first negotiation session, management listed the following contract modifications necessary for the Ohio site to be selected:

1. Eliminate the existing COLA;

2. Limit the definition of overtime to "hours worked in excess of the 40-hour workweek," thus allowing management to schedule plant operations seven days per week without *per se* overtime rates on weekends;

3. Disallow bumping into the new plant when layoffs occurred elsewhere in nearby plants, thus allowing management to avoid potentially costly retraining; disallow bumping *out* of the plant to prevent the loss of valuable training for people seeking higher pay at external locations;

4. Establish a lower day-work rate than had existed in the earlier prototype operations.

Although management remained pessimistic about the likelihood of union members agreeing to these terms, the local president told corporate planners, "Put it on paper and we'll look at it and let you know." The local was given three months to negotiate conditions. Local leadership saw the company's proposal on necessary union concessions as excessive and believed that the excessiveness stemmed, in part, from the desire on one corporate planner's part to have the plant located in Nebraska. At the same time, the local president realized that the location of the Air Spring plant in Ohio represented a rare opportunity for growth for his local. He did not dispute the company's need for concessions. The company, however, seemed to be asking for more than the situation really required.

The company had time to ponder its plant location decision because output expansion was needed only to meet *future* product demand. The state of auto demand in 1982 was sufficiently weak that the company was not under immediate pressure to increase output. The local president participated in a number of relocation discussions with the corporate chairman, the director of industrial relations and a personnel manager involved in the project. International representatives played a significant role in urging the corporation to open negotiations and consider a local plant site, but the local had complete autonomy over the mix of economic or work rule concessions it would accept to win the plant.

The local union had permitted productivity gains through work rule changes and job consolidation during negotiations in prior years. In contrast to some union leaders' hard line positions, the local president had focused on convincing workers to "put in a full day's work for a full day's pay," and thereby justify a higher wage and fringe package. Wage or fringe concessions to ensure the relocation of the Air Spring plant in Ohio would place the local union president in unfamiliar, and potentially tenuous, political circumstances.

Contributing Factors

Both proximity to corporate headquarters and leadership stability within the union favored a heightened awareness of the company's situation by the local union. The local office was located across the street from corporate headquarters and the international union offices were in the same city. Union officials had ready access to corporate executives, up to and including the CEO, and fully exercised these access options. Informal or formal meetings between union and company representatives reportedly took place on a weekly basis—or more frequently.

The local president had been with the corporation for approximately 40 years; the last 15 years of his 26-year tenure as a union officer were spent as president of his local. He was, therefore, familiar with the status of company operations, and he knew that the corporation had closed down plants when lower wages and fringes could not be obtained. He also knew it was unlikely the company would knowingly build a plant in a high wage and high labor cost environment. His long-term knowledge of the company and the industry provided him with an overall perspective that supported, and lent credence to, the company position.

The local union president was not involved in any sort of intraunion political struggle; therefore, he was not pressured into the more militant bargaining stance which is sometimes required to appease the rank and file. Moreover, the local had a set policy for dealing with such situations. According to this policy, union negotiators would make no final decisions. Consequently, members recognized that they would have the ultimate responsibility to approve or disapprove the new settlement.

The management team involved in the plant location decision was centrally located at the corporate headquarters. This factor reduced the chances that intracompany communications would be misconstrued. Furthermore, local managers and corporate headquarters were not competing to meet their respective goals. Finally, as mentioned earlier, corporate leadership had more than an economic interest in the community's economic well-being, since it was "home" to most of them.

Final Outcome

Despite the union's traditional unwillingness to consider wage and fringe concessions and the company's initial predisposition to locate in Nebraska, agreement on modified terms for a new Air Spring plant in a nearby community was finally reached. The plant was built and began operations in January 1981.

The local president was convinced that the existing contract language would have been too costly to bring the plant to Ohio and persuaded members that concessions were in their best interests. The parties agreed to a contract that allowed the newly relocated plant to be exempt from areawide layoff procedures and bumping arrangements. The corporation's original proposal to have a completely independent seniority arrangement was not adopted, however. Laid-off employees from other plants could sign the area hiring list and, if hired, receive credit for prior seniority. Moreover, no bidding out of the Air Spring plant was permitted if job openings became available in other nearby corporate plants. Other management demands concerning scheduling, elimination of COLA, and use of measured day work with no incentives were also met. Operations began with a 90-member workforce. By mid-1985, employment had reached about 200 in the plant.

Inferences

It is difficult to overstate the importance of the international representatives' and local president's proximity to corporate executives, and the concomitant "inside" information that was available to them concerning corporate investment plans. Second, more militant leaders probably would not have learned of the Air Spring expansion plans until it was too late to act effectively. Watching job loss over a period of 10-15 years had taken the abrasive edge off union leaders in this case. For that reason, management, perhaps inadvertently, was willing to let the rumor out concerning the new plant and then pursue negotiations with the local to see whether conditions could be set that would permit the plant to be operated economically in Northeast Ohio.

The political security from which the local president operated gave him the option of pursuing the tactics he did under the circumstances. He could risk voting for the elimination of *per se* Sunday overtime rates at a sister plant and point to that to gain a commitment from the corporate chairman to reconsider the Air Spring plant site. Then he could take the matter of contract modifications for the plant to his executive committee and local membership.

Finally, it is difficult to gauge the significance of the fact that few of those who voted for the "special agreement" on the Air Spring plant actually contemplated working there. Even though some of them might eventually transfer to the plant, most had jobs at other facilities that probably seemed secure at the time of the Air Spring plant negotiations. The special agreement for the Air Spring plant may be analogous to two-tier bargaining to the extent that unrepresented future employees' wages, hours and working conditions were being set in these negotiations. The economic conditions confronting the union and its motivation are also similar. Two-tier bargaining, like the special Air Spring agreement, enhances job opportunity, membership gain, and job security for existing union members.

There are some differences, however. First, the Air Spring agreement was more comprehensive. From the company's standpoint, work rules, seniority bidding, bumping rights and *per se* overtime were at least as important as wage rates in the special agreement at Air Spring. Ordinarily, two-tier settlements discriminate only with respect to wages and, perhaps, to a limited extent, benefits. Second, existing employees have the potential to move into Air Spring and be covered by the revised agreement language.

What Air Spring demonstrates is that "greenfield" operations need not be far removed from existing plant locations in order for companies to take advantage of most of the labor relations motives for starting such operations. Locating them near existing facilities offers management, employees, and unions advantages, as well. To the extent that the advantages for management compensate for the negotiation expense, keeping "greenfield" plants close to the original facility is economically rational.

Timkin Company Steel Mill

This corporation has been family-owned since its inception in St. Louis in 1899. In 1902, it relocated to Canton in Northeast Ohio, in order to be close to the growing automobile industry for which it produced roller bearing axles. In 1915, the company reduced its dependence on suppliers by building its own steel mill in which it produced the highest quality bearing steel. By the 1940s, the corporation had become the major employee in Canton and principal benefactor. Even though the corporation had plants overseas, management spokespersons expressed great loyalty to the community in which their headquarters were located.

The company's steelmaking capacity has always exceeded its own needs for bearing production. Consequently, it has historically sold a portion of its output to other users of high alloy steel—even other bearing producers. In many cases, customers have become dependent on the corporation for their steel supplies. Demand for company bearings in the 1970s, however, grew to a point where well over half of its steel output was being consumed internally and long-term customers were being forced to look elsewhere for supplies. At that point, the company began to explore the expansion of its steel production.

In the course of such investigations, the company discovered a number of technological breakthroughs in steel production that had the potential to enhance quality well beyond what the company could produce in its existing mills. To maintain its position as a world leader in quality steel *and* as a major supplier of such steel, the company developed plans to build a new state-of-the-art mill. Management expected that only about 30 percent of the mill's output would be used internally and that the rest could be available for sale. Plans for the plant were announced early in 1981.

Company Decision

The company's decision to build a new plant was based on considerations of quality and production capacity, similar to the air spring plant of the preceding case. Labor relations issues became relevant only with respect to location. The new technology of the mill required flexibility in assigning work and broader job descriptions than existed in the old facility. Moreover, management could not agree to the same incentive pay program for the new mill.

The company evaluated potential sites in Tennessee and Virginia in addition to a location within several miles of its old mill and corporate headquarters. Unlike Air Spring, management in this case was predisposed to locate the new mill near its headquarters rather than out-of-state for a variety of reasons. The company realized it had a unique leadership role and a high degree of influence in the community—a set of desirable circumstances not easily duplicable elsewhere.

Management's predisposition explains why it initiated discussions with the union concerning contract modifications. (In Air Spring, management had the opposite predisposition and would probably have built its new spring plant in Nebraska had the union not initiated discussions on the matter.)

Union Awaremess

The company notified the union of its intentions and needs and requested a meeting with the union to discuss the issues. It was the belief of the local union president that company interest in locating the plant outside Ohio was only cursory. This belief was shared by other union members, leading the company to include the following statement in an information packet given to its employees:

> Is there any truth to the rumor that the company investigated building the steel mill in the South only to put pressure on us here . . . ?

> There's not a word of truth to that rumor.

The company officially maintained that Northeast Ohio was merely one of several sites being reviewed and that while management would recognize the existing union in the new mill—if a new mill were to be built locally—the union would have to agree to concessions before the local site was selected.

There was little doubt that all factions of the union realized how desirable it would be for the new mill to be located locally. Although the corporation was still hiring in 1981 when the negotiations were taking place, employees were laid off by the hundreds beginning in 1982.

Local union leaders and other union members felt that the company was acting opportunistically. Serious cutbacks in nearby Youngstown and the closure of one steel mill there had set the stage for major concessions in national steel negotiations. Timkin was not part of national negotiations, nor was it facing the same market conditions for its unique products. In the view of union negotiators, it was arguable whether the company needed any substantial union concessions in order to be persuaded to opt for the local mill site. The company, as described by a union spokesperson, had always operated from a position of highly centralized control; plant locations outside the region might lessen headquarters' ability to adequately monitor the new mill's operations.

The local president believed that the corporation was likely to locate the new mill nearby regardless of union concessions. However, neither he nor the international representative cared to take a stance adamantly opposed to concessions only to discover that the company was not bluffing. The new mill would represent 800 new members to the local union and increase job security for all employees.

The package of union concessions, which the corporation claimed was necessary to assure the location of the new steel mill in the area, was not solely confined to operations within the proposed mill. The company also wanted concessions from union members who would continue working in the existing steel plant. These demands led some union members to feel that the company was using the new mill negotiations to back out of its existing labor agreement. Among other demands, the company wanted current employees to agree to give up their incentive premium. Over the years since it was initially installed by the company, the incentive premium plan had resulted in unintended "overpayments" to a number of employees. Naturally, the beneficiaries of these payments were reluctant to give them up.

Decision Process

Historically, the company had assumed the initiator's role in the decision process in labor relations, taking a very formal stance in any of its meetings with the union. All meetings were transcribed, and a company spokesman indicated that no informal off-the-record meetings occurred.

It is not surprising therefore that the corporation was in the "driver's seat" throughout negotiations concerning the new mill location. The first company proposal required the union to make concessions in exchange for *consideration* of Northeast Ohio as a possible site. The union's position was that any concessions on its part would be conditioned on a *decision* to locate the plant in Northeast Ohio.

Wishing to move forward with negotiations, the company agreed to discussions without preconditions in June 1981. Assuming a typically aggressive labor relations stance, company negotiators laid out all their new proposals pertaining to the steel mill site without encouraging any give-and-take process. One item of considerable importance was a no-strike pledge at the new mill site until 1992. The company's position was that regardless of where it was located, it could not afford to have the mill shut down at any time during its initial start-up phase. The company also demanded the elimination of incentive pay at both the new and existing mills. According to the local president's account of the June meeting, neither he nor the international representative interjected any objections to the company's plan. Even corporate insinuations that the union might not act in their members' best interests in this matter were allowed to pass without union comment.

In July 1981, the company proposal was presented by union leaders to their constituency. In the process, however, the company's package was presented to union members in pieces. This approach allowed union members to ratify some, but not all, corporate proposals. Management was angry with the union leaderships' tactics of presentation. It was management's view that union negotiators used these tactics in order to get back to the bargaining table, so management reasserted its control over the bargaining process. About two weeks after partial ratification of the company's proposals, Timkin stated that union leaders must secure ratification of the company package, in its entirety, or another site would be chosen.

A ballot on the entire package was scheduled for October 11, 1981. Again, union leadership, who had not participated in shaping the package, refused to make any recommendation. Union members narrowly rejected it. The local president attributed this result to strong employee opposition to an 11-year contract and elimination of the incentive premium. Any incentive premium concession represented both a loss of income and a loss of face for union negotiators because the company had been trying to eliminate the incentive premium for years. An outside source also asserted that the union leaders made no real effort to explain the company's offer or the potential benefits. He also indicated that the date of October 11 coincided with the Pittsburgh Steelers-Cleveland Browns football game, a scheduling that assured a very low voter turnout.

The second round began almost immediately. Once rejection of the company plan was confirmed, the company mounted a new, intensive strategy to gain worker accceptance of corporate proposals, and outside forces began to assert pressure on both negotiating parties. Management, apparently believing the union's persuasion efforts had been inadequate, initiated direct communications with their employees. Information pamphlets were mailed out, question and answer hotlines were activated, newspaper informational ads were published and radio talks on the steel mill proposal were encouraged by management. Furthermore, the corporation's historic and prominent role in the community prompted the city's mayor to become involved in the steel mill issue. According to the local president, the mayor's participation was critical in maintaining negotiation efforts between the two parties. Without him, the formal distance between the parties may have prevented a resumption of negotiations.

The central message in all of the company's communication efforts was designed to have an impact on union members, their families and the company in general. According to the company, a new steel mill in the area would provide continued job security for current workers and generate desirable employment opportunities for other members of the community.

The company's proposal was again presented to union members for a vote. In addition to community pressure and the company's major communications effort, the company had removed the incentive premium issue from the bargaining table. They agreed to allow existing premium issues to be determined in arbitration. Finally, in a side letter to the international representative, the company agreed that if the package were ratified, they *would* build the plant at the local site. While it is unclear which of the company's actions influenced the workers most significantly, the combined impact of the above-mentioned events led to a union member ratification of the company's package by a 10-to-1 ratio. By mid-1982, the plant was under construction.

Contributing Factors

A number of factors may have had a significant bearing on the negotiations for the new steel plant. First, and possibly foremost, it appears that the company perceives a local location as advantageous. Because they want a high degree of corporate control over operations, management favored a steel mill site located near corporate headquarters. Moreover, the company has great influence within the community, as was illustrated by the union president's statement, ''The Corporation owns the town.'' Community leaders are likely to be more responsive here to the needs of the company than in other cities.

The local union does not have a history of ''bucking the company.'' The corporation is, and historically has been, tough on the issue of management rights. Union members appear to have generally accepted the company's dominant role. The last major strike occurred in 1968. A brief 1986 strike did not affect the new mill. The company has also experienced a low level of grievances and arbitration.

Moreover, there was some lack of harmony within the union bargaining team. Lack of internal union cohesiveness allowed the company to assume a leadership position in the bargaining process. Divided union leadership also allowed the company to mobilize its forces effectively to influence union members directly and to mount an effective public relations program without an effective countervailing union effort.

By contrast, management's structure and policies enhanced internal consonance. Family members own and operate the company, leaving them relatively free to develop their bargaining position with little out-side interference. Presidents of the company have been knowledgeable on labor relations matters and have, over the years, played major roles in labor negotiations. Even though the president did not sit in negotia-tions for the new mill, the union was well aware of his behind-the-scene role.

Finally, it is clear that community leaders wanted the new steel mill to be built in the area. While local city leaders never explicitly stated as much, they may have presented the community with a perception that "a vote against the company's proposal is a vote against the com-munity." At the very least, the community believed its economic future was linked to the corporation's prosperity.

Final Outcome

The agreement between the two parties, effective November 1981, reflected the bargaining strength of the company. Wages and condi-tions of employment were positive from a managerial point of view. The contractual provision allowing the company complete hiring discre-tion was also significant. At will, management was free to obtain new steel mill employees from internal or external labor pools. A two-tiered wage settlement was negotiated so that new employees would receive a lower rate of compensation than current employees in comparable positions in both the old mill and the new one.

The company also obtained a favorable agreement concerning con-tract length and contract renewal conditons for the new plant. The original contract would be in operation for three years. Prior to the end of the three-year period, either party could indicate a desire to renegotiate the terms of the contract. If new terms could not be mutually agreed upon, the contract in its original form would be automatically renewed for another three-year period. Two renewals of this nature would be allowed. In other words, the company was assured that no strike would occur at the new plant for this entire period. (The agreement for the existing plant was not subject to the same automatic renewal provisions.)

After this nine-year period, the existing plant and the new steel mill would jointly negotiate a contract. Even at this point, the company re-tained a written understanding that the new plant's agreement might contain additional unique provisions.

Included in the initial contract were provisions allowing for considerable managerial flexibility in job assignments, grievance processing and layoffs during the mill "construction period" (considered to extend three years past the first production of steel). For example, during this rather lengthy time period, the union would not be permitted to grieve any corporate action related to: (1) hiring or layoff of new employees, (2) selection, assignment, and qualifications of employees, whether newly hired or transferred, (3) the work to be performed, and (4) the return of employees to their previous occupations.

Seniority rights, incentive plans and numerous other wage and working conditions were also considerably reduced or designed to allow for a high degree of managerial flexibility. Furthermore, each contract provision could remain in place through three contract periods, should management choose not to agree to a contractual change proposed by the union.

Inferences

The relative power of the company in these negotiations is clear, but it is not readily apparent why the union constituency was so overwhelmingly persuaded to the company's position. Skepticism concerning both the company's intentions to locate elsewhere and its genuine need for concessions was expressed at both the leader and rank-and-file levels.

Some appreciation of the temporal and spatial context might be helpful. At the time of negotiations, plant closings had caused the international representative in this case to have lost more than half his membership. Local workers were clearly aware of these circumstances. No matter how small the risk of losing the plant, no one on the union side was inclined to take it.

Furthermore, Timkin is not generally regarded by its employees with the same negative passion that is expressed by some militant workers and union leaders. The local president himself expressed the view at several points during the interview that the corporation is a good place to work. This unusually high degree of trust in management (not because the company is regarded as benevolent, but because the managers are perceived as good businessmen) probably accounts for the overwhelming vote on the company proposal.

Whether the company's willingness to return to negotiations after the initial rejection points to patience in dealing with the union, or simply points to the absence of any intent to consider alternative locations will never be known. In any event, in this case where the company's demands were primarily directed at an unknown group of employees (the workforce of the new mill), where the temporal and spatial environment favored easy ratification, and where a history of cooperative union reponse to management prevailed, the negotiations were not easy.

Conclusion

Air Spring and Timkin vividly illustrate the time frame relevant for a discussion of plant closure. For a union representative, no time is too early to think about the factors that cause plants to close. Since every plant will eventually close, it is essential to secure new investment, on site or nearby, that will assure job security for union members.

Knowledge or information about corporate plans is, of course, the *sine qua non* for success in securing new plants. In Air Spring, such information appears to have been obtained fortuitously. The quality of the local union president's relationship with management representatives who could tell him about the corporation's Air Spring plans cannot be ignored, however. Had the relationship been strained, it is unlikely the information would have been exchanged.

At Timkin, the company initiated the dialogue for several apparent reasons. It wanted to locate the new mill in the Canton area; it saw that the agreement revisions it needed to operate the plant efficiently would not be terribly onerous to the steelworkers union; and it recognized that in the economic climate of 1980-81, when nearly half the steelworker jobs in the area, including nearly all of them in Youngstown, had been eliminated, it could approach these negotiations from a position of power.

Union negotiators in both cases were prepared to discuss inducements they might offer in the form of agreement modifications. The companies had alternatives with respect to plant location. Key union negotiators knew it, and feared that an alternative to Northeast Ohio might be selected for the new plant. Perhaps even more important, both unions had experienced job loss due to plant closure so that job security had greater priority than it might otherwise have had in earlier times.

Finally, the union negotiators in both cases were able to agree because rank-and-file resistance to company demands was not organized or significant. At Timkin, the key issue was an incentive pay plan that the company wanted to remove, not only at the new mill but in the old one as well. Once this issue was withdrawn by the company, at least insofar as the old mill was concerned, the agreement was overwhelmingly ratified.

Perhaps the most difficult element in negotiations of this type is the fact that existing employees, and their representatives, do not necessarily see that the location of a new plant nearby is worth anything to them. In fairness, recognition of a tragedy scenario like Truck Components is difficult without hindsight. Why should existing workers, with some seniority, give up favorable terms of employment when there is no immediate tangible benefit? Only if the new plant is seen by the employees as insurance against the tragedy scenario will they be willing to "pay" for it. Even in the cases included here, it is not clear that the typical rank-and-file voter saw the ratification of agreement changes in that light.

Union negotiators have a twofold task in such situations. First, they must be assured, themselves, that there is an "insurance" payoff for their members. Not all new plants will assure the development of jobs of comparable quality or that their existing members will be in line to obtain the jobs. Then, leaders must educate members with respect to the *quid pro quo*. Employers cannot be expected to give up tangible benefits for an intangible promise. The general economic climate of Northeast Ohio, as well as the industries involved, helped secure the new plants in these cases. When the circumstances are less favorable to rank-and-file acceptance, union leaders will have a more difficult task.

NOTE

1. The name of the corporation has been withheld at the request of the company.

5
Findings and Conclusions
Some Private and Public Alternatives

Although it is difficult and possibly misleading to draw broad, general conclusions out of a handful of case studies, the usefulness of a project such as this would be limited without such an attempt. Readers are, of course, free to draw their own conclusions based on the principal findings summarized below.

General Findings and Conclusions

Why Plants Close

When viewed from a short run perspective, it is clear that market conditions drive *bona fide* plant closure negotiations. If market forces are strong enough, there is no hope for saving a plant. All three cases of chapter 2—Blue Water Seafood, Custom Lumber Products, and Truck Components—illustrate this.

In the case of Custom Lumber Products, a sudden change in the market for complementary factors of production, namely, transportation costs, caused the plant to become unprofitable. Its continued operation could not be justified. Truck Components and Blue Water Seafood closed because of changes in the market for the product produced. For Blue Water Seafood, consumer preference shifted away from the products. At Truck Components, the introduction of competitive suppliers into the marketplace from Japan had a devastating effect. Corporate market share was drastically reduced and consolidation of its production into more efficient facilities was necessary.

A common characteristic of all three cases was the narrow range of products being produced and the absence of new products or production technology that might have kept the plant competitive. In two of the three cases, the facilities were less than 15 years old at the time of closure; so an obsolete plant, in itself, was not a factor in their closure.

It would be inappropriate to conclude that the absence of new products or new technology always leads to plant closure in the short run or, conversely, that their introduction always saves plants. It seems reasonable to conclude though, that product diversity and new technology do enhance a plant's life expectancy.

High labor costs or a poor labor climate were not blamed by management for the closure of any of the three plants discussed in chapter 2. This is not to say that labor climate was irrelevant. In fact, with respect to Truck Components, which was a victim of the "tragedy scenario," the poor labor climate and high labor costs of the 1950s were what led directly to the corporation's decision to invest in plants in other parts of the country. Without realizing it at the time, the corporation placed the future of the Cleveland Truck Components plant in jeopardy when these new plants were built elsewhere. At all three plants discussed in chapter 2, a better labor climate might have encouraged investment in new technologies or new product lines at the Cleveland plants, so that when the product market in one line failed, others would have been there to absorb the shock.

One might argue that although the preceding conclusion is reasonable, it has doubtful value. Neither unions nor management had much concern for labor climate in the 1950s. Why concern ourselves with spilled milk? Even though some unions were willing to make concessions at the time closures were announced in the late 1970s and early 1980s, the opportunities for improving the labor climate and unit labor cost pattern had long passed.

On the other hand, there is an apparent lesson for surviving managers, employees, and unions: pressure must be continually applied to bring new products and new technologies into an existing plant. Products and plants have a finite "life cycle." As those from the marketing field will attest, a product life cycle can be extended by various means. It seems clear from this study that intervention will also have an effect on "plant life cycles" as well. Constant attention to the labor climate as well as corporate investment decisions would undoubtedly have an impact on the life expectancy of a plant. Such a finding is consistent with that of Anil Verma that unions have no choice but to negotiate for more new investment.[1]

Can Plants be Saved Through Negotiations?

A second conclusion that seems justified on the basis of the four cases in chapter 3 is that where the threat to the plant's survival stems, in part, from high unit labor costs, collective bargaining can be an effective way to address the situation. The cases demonstrate that a poor industrial relations climate can be changed, and that by changing such a climate plants can be saved from premature closure. Just as death can be held off by timely medical treatment, so too can plants be saved, at least for a time, with joint problem solving, provided both parties genuinely desire a nonfatal solution and discover the problem early enough to take effective action.

A third conclusion, also apparent from the cases in this study, is that various constraints and preconditions for negotiations which are imbedded in the collective bargaining relationship affect the probability of success in reversing the drift toward plant closure. Personal characteristics or aspirations, interpersonal relationships, mutual trust and respect, among others, all seem to have potential to influence the outcome. Although this study has recognized that the economic environment is crucial for determining the range of possible outcomes for any particular plant, its focus has been on the impact "institutional elements" have on the success of plant saving negotiations. The research questions posed in chapter 1 help to frame an outline for the following discussion.

Further Elaboration on the
Plant Closing Negotiations Model

1. *How do unions know when the employer's threat to close is bona fide?* In every case investigated for this study, including those of chapter 2 where the plants were closed, the employer has been willing to discuss candidly the financial circumstances of the particular facility. For some union officials, the accounting data were significant and had an effect on their conclusions concerning the operation of the facility. Many union representatives, as well as their constituents, however, were not persuaded by "the data." Their view was that accounting practices are so sophisticated, and accounting standards are sufficiently nebulous in areas such as cost accounting, that even professional financial analysts might differ with respect to the basic financial condition of a particular operation.

Moreover, an accurate conclusion with respect to the financial performance of an operation may not be the critical indicator anyway. Even profitable operations are sometimes closed when profit rates do not meet corporate minimum expectations or simply because of corporate decisions to "downsize" in response to market changes. The underlying question is whether a facility fits into overall corporate plans in the short to intermediate term of two to five years. The answer may depend on a variety of factors related to the facility's financial performance, but is not determined by it.

Rather than financial performance, the more critical indicators of management's intentions relate to maintenance and housekeeping, new product and technology innovation in a facility, and the status of the stock on the shelves. In the words of one union representative, "If employees in the plant just open their eyes, they can tell whether their plant is in trouble."

In some cases, considerable effort was made to persuade union leaders that management truly intended to close the plant unless changes were made. The more difficult educational challenge, however, was that faced by union leaders when they confronted their members. In larger facilities, even though key leaders were convinced the threat was *bona fide*, a substantial segment of the rank and file was not convinced. As noted in the case of Auto Parts, most of the bargaining committee was sufficiently ambivalent that they refused to take a position on the work rules concession package. In addition, more radical political activists accused the local president of being the "concession king" and implied that he was betraying the interests of the rank and file. Such a difference of opinion among those who are closest to the situation and who have the most at stake suggests that there is no reliable way to determine whether an employer threat to close is *bona fide* or not. In smaller facilities, the problem was not as severe apparently because members had the same exposure to information and other indicators of the company's condition as their leaders had.

2. *Why does an employer initiate discussions?* There have been NLRB and court decisions relating to the employer's obligation to bargain in the context of plant closing.[2] Based on managerial interviewees' reports for this project, however, legal pressure was not a significant factor in management's desire to discuss potential plant closing in any of the cases studied.

One surprising finding was that employers tend not to be dissuaded from attempting negotiations with a union concerning the preservation of a plant when there has been a history of difficult labor-management relations. The history of the relationship may be important in determining *how* the employer approaches these negotiations, though. In the context of difficult labor-management relations, employers tend to assume more rigid "take it or leave it" attitudes. Typical among those following such a pattern was the Auto Parts plant. Even where management opens with a firm position, however, such as in the case of Ohio Rubber, where a two-dollar cut in labor costs was demanded, negotiations typically lead to compromise.

In a case where plant closure was not explicitly raised as an issue by management, Wrapping Materials, there was no attempt by management to conceal its intentions with respect to the plant. In fact, management revealed its long-term corporate investment program to a meeting of the employees in that plant and it was that corporate investment program presentation that led to discussions between the plant manager and the union.

Even in Blue Water Seafood, where there was no significant discussion with the union concerning keeping the plant open, the absence of discussion was *not* due to any attempt by management to keep the union in the dark. Management indicated to the union that such discussions would be fruitless in light of its product market analysis which had nothing to do with labor costs or climate.

The employer who raises the issue of possible plant closing for discussion seems to do so when several critical factors are present. Perhaps most important, the employer must believe there is a realistic possibility of achieving sufficient labor cost savings to justify maintaining the facility. Negotiations to achieve contract modification are typically long and difficult. Despite the perceptions of some union representatives and employees to the contrary, it is unlikely that an employer engages in concession bargaining in order to reduce labor costs for the short run—between the time of such concessions and ultimate closure.

The Truck Components case is one in which the employees and their union leaders expressed special cynicism with regard to management's motives. In that case, after long negotiations, contract modifications were introduced in order to save the Truck Components plant. After the parties reached a settlement, the market for Truck Components' products further deteriorated to the point where the corporation could not justify keeping the plant open. The employees expressed the view that management's motives from the beginning were suspect. It is clear, however, that the investment in the negotiations as well as the costs incurred by management to finance the job guarantees after closure, were substantial and could have been avoided if management had not undertaken negotiations at all. The Truck Components case is one where management incorrectly anticipated the state of the market for its product. It is apparent from this study that when management reaches a decision to close a facility, it does so without raising the question of concessions with the union. The case of Blue Water Seafood illustrates this.

Another important factor that motivates management to raise the question of plant closure in a timely fashion is the commitment of local management to the community in which the plant is located. This factor is difficult to measure and easy to miss in any study of plant closure. It is easy to discount statements by managers that they have a concern for the well-being of long-term employees at a plant, but the evidence in this study suggests that such concern is a factor which affects the effort they are willing to invest in negotiations. Commitment to the community is not altogether altruistic because the managers, themselves, live in the community and are often closely attached to it. In all but one of the nine cases reported in this study, top local management reported that they identified Northeast Ohio as their home. None of them was looking forward to a transfer to some other location if the plant were to close. In other words, there was more than a "corporate interest" from the management side to save the facility.

3. *What factors influence the union response?* In the cases selected for study in this project, negotiations to save plants actually occurred or the union was prepared to engage in such negotiations. Hence, these cases represent only a "tail of the distribution" and are not representative of all plant closing situations. Even so, the responses of the unions varied considerably across cases and over time within cases.

For example, in the case of Cleveland Twist Drill, the union's initial response to the demands made by management to forestall closing were essentially negative. Cleveland Twist Drill is instructive because it represents a case where the employees and the union had been exposed to a number of "facts" that should have convinced them that management was not bluffing. By the time management approached the union for discussions on contract modifications, nearly half of the exempt workforce had been terminated and the union was aware that management had begun the process of expanding production in other locations outside of Cleveland.

In the case of Auto Parts, the local union president favored negotiating and modifying the contract on the terms specified by management, but all of the other members of the union's bargaining team opposed this move by the union. This was in spite of their knowledge that management had excess capacity and that profitability had been eroded substantially because of Japanese imports.

At the other extreme, the union in Wrapping Materials was willing to participate in contract discussions from the time the matter was first raised by management, and to do so in a flexible way. At Ohio Rubber, the pattern was "mixed." That is, the local union president agreed to discussions with the company concerning contract modifications, especially when it was possible that work could be moved back into the plant from a southern location, but when the matter was to be brought before the local union membership for discussion and a vote, the president was reluctant to pursue the matter.

The single ingredient that seems most important in explaining these variations in union leader behavior is "politics." Where union leaders are politically secure, or where they have little regard for their political futures, they seem to be more willing to engage in aggressive discussions with management and to take the lead with respect to proposing changes to their membership. Although with hindsight it is possible to conclude that the leaders in most of the cases made popular decisions with respect to contract modifications and plant preservation, they did not have the advantage of such hindsight at the time they engaged in their negotiations. The membership element has been noted elsewhere. Thomas W. Miner, vice-president for labor relations at Chrysler, noted with respect to 1982 negotiations, "Industry's problems at the bargaining table are not now with union leadership, but with rank and file."[3] Anyone facing plant closure threats must recognize this factor and its influence.

Another factor that appears important is the degree to which the union leaders and their constituents share a cynical attitude toward management. At the initial stages of negotiations, an attitude among the rank and file, and in some cases among the leadership, is that management's sole intention is to "screw the workers." Those who shared this attitude tended to see labor-management negotiations very narrowly as a game in which one side attempts to inflict as much pain and suffering on the other as possible. With that attitude, the question of plant closure was not seen as having the significance that it deserved. It was just one more way that management could attempt to manipulate its bargaining power relative to the union. From this perspective, the response on the union side was naturally to resist any proposals by management and, as much as possible, "to take them down with us when we go."

Such an attitude was not prevalent among the cases we studied, although it clearly plays some role in almost any plant closing negotiation situation. It has to be overcome with appeals to the economic self-interest of the individual workers or it is likely to lead to plant closure.

An alternative for unions when they are confronted with a potential plant closing situation is to turn to third party political action in order to forestall the closing or to apply pressure to the company to reconsider its decision. This kind of action is typical in Europe, as has been noted elsewhere.[4] In this study, there were no cases in which a union attempted to use third party political pressure as a weapon against management. Rather, the union at Cleveland Twist Drill used the political connections it had in order to obtain information and to gather a clearer understanding of the factual situation it faced. Perhaps the most sophisticated use of third party political clout came in the case of Wrapping Materials where the district director of the union worked with the mayor, county leaders, state legislators, and members of Congress to obtain funding and other necessary political decisions that permitted investment to take place. Governmental action to assist in the investment decision there was probably as important as the modification to the labor agreement in the preservation of that plant.

In summary, the political circumstances and aspirations of the union leadership play a significant role in the union's response to an initiative on the part of management to close a plant or to discuss a potential plant closure. Next in importance is the general attitude of the rank and file, or a significant minority within it, toward management and the collective bargaining process. Only where employees see their own economic self-interest as paramount are negotiations likely to proceed effectively. Finally, although they are not an essential element in saving plants, the external political forces that unions can bring to bear can be helpful. At least they were so here, where they were used in a conciliatory way to help overcome the problems faced by management as well as the union.

4. *What are the distinguishing characteristics of successful negotiations?* Two of the important ingredients for success have already been discussed. Union leaders, *and their constituents,* must have access to the facts, and the capacity to understand the economic reality faced by their plant, or the objectives of management with respect to their plant, so that they can negotiate over modifications in contract terms from a realistic position. Second, union leaders must be in politically stable

positions so they can act as industrial statesmen rather than political opportunists.

A third ingredient for success relates to an area only briefly discussed to this point. Union leaders must recognize and take advantage of all the options available to them during plant saving negotiations over contract modifications. The most important issue in plant closing negotiations is job security. In many instances, union leaders are tempted to demand job guarantees, severance pay, or mandatory minimum advance notice of plant shut down. It is not at all clear that these are the demands, even when won, that really protect plants and jobs.

Managerial concessions that insure investment in new technology and new products for the plant are the ones that save plants. There are legal issues here which complicate the matter. Clearly, negotiation concerning investment, product mix, and similar matters are beyond the scope of mandatory issues under the law.[5] Yet, company decisions regarding these matters determine the job security of the employees. In every case in this study where plants have remained open, management has made the commitment to increase investment in the plant or to return jobs to the plant that they had previously located elsewhere or contracted out.

It is clear that union leaders play a crucial role in the question of whether negotiations will be successful, but management has an equally important part to play. With respect to information, management has the capacity to enlighten or to obfuscate with respect to the facts of the matter. To the extent that management chooses the latter course, it is impossible to create the enlightenment necessary on the part of union leaders or their constituents that is critical for the success of negotiations. With respect to the political ingredient, management has the potential to mislead the ''industrial statesman'' union leader, to embarrass such a leader after he has taken the risk to make contract modifications, and so to undermine him that his successor ''knows better'' than ever to trust management again. No matter what the rationale for the U.S. Steel's purchase of Marathon Oil after the Steelworkers agreed to concessions, the union leaders and their members felt duped. The political embarrassment has clearly led union leaders to make statements and to take positions that might otherwise be considered irrational.

In all four successful cases investigated for this study, management followed through, in letter and, more important, in spirit, with respect to commitments they made at the bargaining table. At Cleveland Twist Drill, the company increased the number of jobs beyond any agreement to do so. At Auto Parts, the company has increased beyond its commitments both the number of jobs and the investment in new tools and equipment. Such moves by management clearly reinforce the decisions made by the industrial statesman union leader when the contract modifications were agreed upon. They also make it possible for other industrial statesmen to emerge.

Finally, the willingness of management to discuss nonmandatory issues at the bargaining table enables union leaders to negotiate for terms that provide true job security—more investment in technology and new products for the plant. Management's reactions to union demands for increased investment will help existing employees to see that their own job security is a function of company growth at their location.

Private Policy Alternatives

The findings of this study have implications for both policy and strategic planning on the question of plant closing. This section deals first with the decision model and factors that might be considered in an employer decision concerning the closure of a plant. It then considers the strategies that are likely to be most useful from a union standpoint.

An Employer Decision Model

When an employer considers closing a plant, it may be motivated by a desire to *reduce* overall production or a decision to *move* the production to what the employer believes is a more efficient location elsewhere. Such a decision to move may be the result of an earlier decision to reduce overall production which, in turn, caused capacity utilization in a number of different facilities to become less than optimal. Consolidation of production into a smaller number of locations, sometimes called "rationalization," promises more efficient operations.

A decision to move production may also be motivated by the promise of a better labor climate including lower labor costs. Even where a decision to move production to another location and close a Cleveland facility was motivated solely by desire to consolidate, the alternative of closing the distant location and retaining the Cleveland site is also a possible alternative—one that would presumably be considered if the labor climate or labor cost picture in Cleveland were bright.[6]

As noted in the earlier part of this chapter, a decision to close based on an immediate need to reduce production is irreversible, regardless of union response. Blue Water Seafood illustrated such a situation. When closure is the result of consolidation or rationalization of production into more productive facilities after production levels have been reduced, e.g. Truck Components, no union response is likely to be effective either. In both of these cases, market conditions overwhelm any consideration that might be given to labor climate. When closure is considered specifically because of a poor labor climate or where two facilities are similar with respect to "technical considerations," i.e., they are technologically comparable and have similar proximity to customers and suppliers, a change in labor climate would likely have an impact on the decision to close.

The following discussion relates to cases where labor climate is relevant. In that context, there appear to be three dimensions to a managerial decision concerning the closure of a particular facility. These are capital investment, continuing operating costs, and noneconomic considerations.

Capital Investment. Ordinarily a decision to relocate production, either by moving to avoid a poor labor climate or to consolidate into a more efficient location, involves capital investment. In the case of Truck Components, this factor was a key element in the local plant manager's strategy to save his plant. In addition to the actual cost of moving tools and equipment to a new location, there is the cost of preparing a receiving site. There may also be severance pay benefits to employees at the site being closed as well as contractual commitments to suppliers at the existing site.

Such capital investments must be amortized over a period of time. In most companies, a rational decision on whether to move production would be subject to the same constraints as any other capital investment decision. That is, the investment in a move would have to meet corporate threshold payback or return on investment (ROI) criteria. Payback or return on investment would be measured in terms of the savings that flow from continuing operations after the move has been made versus the costs of continued operations at the existing location. These savings are, of course, estimated prior to a move and subject to uncertainty.

An alternative capital investment for the company might be the expenditure of executive time to negotiate with the union to improve the labor climate and reduce labor costs in the existing location. This is the approach Truck Components attempted to use. Such an investment might be substantial in order to assure success. It is also made at some risk because it is difficult to determine in advance that a substantial expenditure of executive time and talent will yield a lower cost labor climate. In any event it may be possible to compare the capital investment of moving versus the investment by management in creating a new labor climate at the existing location. It is conceivable that the latter will reflect lower overall cost for the corporation than the former, so that if comparable cost savings can be attained by either means, an investment in improving the labor climate may be the better choice.

The same analysis also applies to a decision where outright closure rather than a move is contemplated. That is, there may be situations where the "exit cost" to the firm of a shutdown is greater than the required investment to improve labor climate to a level where continued operations produce profits in excess of threshold ROI.

Operating Costs. The savings that flow from a lower per unit operating cost at a new or consolidated location are the returns to an investment that might justify a move. In many cases, it is possible to identify a more efficient location than the existing plant. Simply identifying a more efficient location is not adequate to justify a move, however. The difference in savings must be sufficient to pay back the capital investment (with interest) that is necessary to finance the move. An accurate estimate of capital investment necessary to finance a move is possible. The estimation of continuing operating costs at the new location is more difficult. Unless a company already has experience in a given market with both the quality and cost of labor, it is difficult to know what the nature of the labor market will be in the new location.

It is, of course, necessary to compare the projected costs at the new location with estimated costs at the existing location after an investment in improving the labor climate has been made. It may well be that the operating costs at the new location would be no lower than they might be at the existing location after such an investment in improving the labor climate has been made.

Noneconomic Considerations. Although the above analysis implicitly includes among the capital and operating costs the time spent by management in labor-management relations and improving the labor climate, there are elements that cannot be included in the economic analysis. Among these are the personal preferences of management for a location in which to live. In general, this study has found that such preferences work to the advantage of a decision to maintain a local facility rather than close and move to a new location. There are, of course, examples to the contrary where local Cleveland companies have been relocated to the Sunbelt apparently at the insistence of top management who had a preference to move to the new location. There are also external political considerations that have motivated company relocation. Where a political climate is not conducive to local corporate interests, there may be an inclination to move.

Finally, the preference of some employers to avoid dealing with unions "at any cost" must also be taken into consideration. Some employers have a nonrational (from an economic standpoint) view that managing without unions is always preferable to managing with them. Under such circumstances, a decision to move for the purpose of avoiding unions cannot be overcome by investment in improving the labor climate. Several Cleveland corporations, including one company that was included in this study, have expressed an explicit policy of investing only in new locations where unions can be avoided. This is not to say that they are specifically engaging in the tactic of the "runaway shop," but it is implicit, pursuant to the tragedy scenario, that such a policy would lead to the loss of plants in the Cleveland area as production rationalization occurs into newer more efficient facilities outside of the Cleveland area.[7]

Union Policy

A union's response to threatened plant closure appears to be the result, in part, of the general perception its leadership holds with respect to the commercial/industrial world. A number of interviewees, particularly the dissident, more radical union leaders who were interviewed in this project, expressed a view of management that was cynical and negative. It was their view that management success depended entirely on the extent to which employees could be exploited. This perception of management led union leaders to think of negotiations in the context of a threatened closure as entirely distributive. Another element of this view is that so-called plant saving negotiations have nothing to do with saving plants. That is, employers engage in such negotiations to exact concessions from the workforce either to reduce the costs of operating a plant already targeted for closure *or* to bluff a union into accepting long-term labor cost cuts at a facility that would continue in operation in any event.

The tactical position of labor negotiators who held such views was to resist any form of contract modification at the bargaining table. Unfortunately, where management has made a *bona fide* threat to close a facility, and the possibility for saving it is tied directly to labor cost and climate considerations, such a tactical position is fatal.

An alternative view among a much larger group of labor negotiators was that management merely acts opportunistically in the context of difficult economic times. Their view was that management faced alternative production location decisions and made them on the basis of relative costs. For these negotiators, the tactical position was altogether different. The key question was at what labor cost level would management actually close the facility or retain it. The answer to some of these questions was obviously difficult to obtain since management was not altogether clear in its own mind on this issue in some of the negotiations, especially where the state of the product market was uncertain. Moreover, such labor negotiators were also faced with the question of what level of wages and benefits their membership would ratify.

To varying degrees, the labor negotiators who fit this model might be referred to as "industrial statesmen." They tended to be less opportunistic themselves with respect to the political environment within their unions. They were not necessarily altruistic in their views, but recognized that the long-run interests of their union and themselves lay in a careful investigation of the position management was taking at the bargaining table. The action model employed by these pragmatic labor leaders was to seek more information and ultimately to attain commitments from management that would assure job security for their members through greater investment or the introduction of new products in the plants that were threatened with closure.

When to Talk About Saving Plants. McKersie[8] has concluded that union consultation (meaning access, influence and involvement) at top corporate levels was a necessary ingredient for saving plants. That is, unless unions are allowed access to the "strategic" level of corporate decisionmaking, there is little hope they can influence plant closing decisions.

This study is consistent with McKersie's conclusions so long as a broad definition of "access" is employed. Unions obtained access in numerous ways in these cases, but typically *through* local management. Initial discussions regarding future corporate plans occurred at that level. Only subsequently, with encouragement and support from local management, were the unions able to access top management. Possible exceptions to this conclusion were Air Spring and Timkin, where new plant location decisions were involved, but also where top corporate management was located in the same community as local union leadership. It is not clear which of these factors led Air Spring and Timkin to be exceptional cases.

Power vs. Reason. Power in a bargaining relationship is the ability to impose costs on the other party. The irony in plant closing negotiations is that the exercise of power by a union is almost sure to be fatal.

Power is the *means* to obtain the attention of top management, however. The ability to drive up the cost of moving work or, perhaps more important, to lower the cost of retaining a plant, causes top management to listen more intently to what a union has to say. Ultimately, economic reason must drive any plant closing decision, however, so union negotiators must be prepared to rely on it once they come to the bargaining table.

Public Policy Implications

The American model of union-management relations has been characterized as "legalistic" relative to most other industrial relations systems in developed economies. Since the Wagner Act was passed in 1935, the parties have relied on the government to define the nature of their relationship. This has been especially true with respect to the scope of bargaining—the range of subjects about which the parties are obligated to negotiate. Section 8(d) of the National Labor Relations Act (NLRA) obligated employers to negotiate only with respect to "wages, hours, and other terms and conditions of employment." By mutual agreement other issues could be negotiated, but employers were not obligated to negotiate with respect to them, and unions were forbidden to apply coercive economic pressure, e.g., the strike, to press their demands in these areas. In general, corporate investment decisions, decisions to open or close plants, and related "strategic" managerial issues are *not mandatory* subjects of bargaining.[9] This study suggests that the potential for saving plants through negotiations might be enhanced if national labor policy was modified with respect to plant closing and, more important, investment decisions.

Plant Closure

At the present time, the law provides only that an employer must negotiate the impact of a closure, not the closure itself, unless the closure decision "turns on" labor costs (the "*Otis Elevator* rule"). Even though such "effects" bargaining obligations may require some notice of the closing decision,[10] it does not require the same advance warning that a "decision" bargaining right would require.[11]

Moreover, the *Otis Elevator* rule may be difficult to interpret and enforce because it requires a determination of motive, i.e., that the employer decision turns on labor costs, before the obligation to bargain is clear. As noted throughout the cases analyzed in this study, the decision to close is almost always related to *profitability*. Labor cost is one element in such a calculation. From an economic viewpoint, to say that a decision is based on other elements determining profitability, but not on labor costs, would be equivalent to arguing that the upper blade of the proverbial scissors cuts while the bottom one does not.

A more productive line of reasoning for the adjudication of this issue would flow from the Supreme Court's rule in *National Woodwork Manufacturer's Association v. NLRB* (386 US 612, 1967), i.e., that work preservation and job security go to the heart of a union's *raison d'etre*, thus matters relating to such issues are mandatory. From such a conclusion, one could argue that *any* plant closure *decision* is mandatory.

From a pragmatic standpoint, if public policy is intended to facilitate saving plants and jobs, this study supports the idea that demands for *contractual rules* relating to plant closure should be mandatory. For successful negotiations to occur with respect to saving a plant, a union must have some timely notice that a decision to close is under consideration. None of the evidence collected for this study suggests that such prior notice to the union, where it has been negotiated into the labor agreement, has been burdensome to the employer. Further study of the use of voluntarily negotiated plant closure notice and its impact on the potential for saving jobs should be undertaken.

In the absence of such studies, it seems apparent from this study that public policy should encourage the negotiation of notice requirements and the opportunity for the union to have an impact on decisions to close plants before such decisions are made. It is not at all clear that such a right for the union can be effectively legislated, but bilateral negotiation of such union rights would have more likelihood for success in the American context. To that end, plant closure clauses, including union demands for advance notice or a right to present alternatives, should be mandatory issues of bargaining. Of course, since the duty to bargain under the NLRA does not require the employer to agree, such a policy would not require employer concessions where the employer believed such concessions would cause serious harm to its ability to operate.

Investment Decisions

As noted above, decisions by the company with respect to investment in new plant or equipment currently are beyond the purview of the mandatory list of subjects for collective bargaining under the NLRA. Investment decisions may be voluntarily negotiated, of course, and, as discussed below, this study illustrates that. The proposal here is parallel with that concerning plant closing. The proposal is not that all investment decisions should be mandatory subjects of bargaining. Rather, a union demand for a contract clause concerning investment should be a mandatory issue. The parties would then be free to develop a contractual agreement that fits their needs. Where management fears that such a clause would be harmful to its interests, it would not be required to agree to any type of investment clause.

The legal effect of the proposed policy change is significant. Under present law, when a company voluntarily negotiates on and agrees to a permissive subject, that subject is not automatically converted into a mandatory subject. Although unilateral change in the clause might be subject to arbitral adjudication, such change might not be illegal under the NLRA, even during the term of an agreement.[12] Thus, such voluntarily negotiated clauses do not provide the same measure of protection as they would if the subject were mandatory.[13] Hence, the possibility for union influence on job security would be substantially enhanced if it had the right to negotiate with management concerning investment decisions.

As noted above, including within the mandatory scope of bargaining the right to negotiate about investment decisions would, in no way compel management to agree to union proposals. On the other hand, it might well be worth considering concessions in this area if a union were willing to modify its position with respect to other terms and conditions in return for such commitments. On a voluntary basis, several of the companies in this study made agreements with respect to new investment, from new production lines to an entire steel mill, in return for changes in work rules, wages, and benefits. Although this pattern is possible in the existing legal context, making investment decisions mandatory would enhance the opportunity for unions to discuss these matters with employers universally, not merely with enlightened management. It would also assure unions legal as well as contractual recourse in the event that management reneged.

The case for a modification in labor law that would make investment decisions a mandatory issue in bargaining is strengthened by a consideration of the pace of technological change in our society, the extent to which new products and new technologies are being introduced, the rapid change in the structure of markets with the increase in international competition, the change in market strength due to deregulation within the economy, and other environmental changes that could be enumerated. The employment uncertainty and insecurity over the last decade, especially with respect to manufacturing, suggests that any union constrained to the traditional narrow scope of bargaining wages, hours and working conditions is likely to be less effective than it could be in representing the long-term security interests of its members.

Conclusion

From a realist's point of view, one might argue that converting investment and plant closing decisions from permissive to mandatory issues would have little effect in the absence of sufficient economic power on the part of unions to achieve inroads at the bargaining table. One might argue that public policy decisions with respect to mandatory subjects of bargaining really have no effect on bargaining behavior.

There is no presumption here that decisions or even legislation in this area will have dramatic effects. As with any complex issue, no simple one-step answer will achieve much. At the margin, however, public policy change does influence the balance of power, and changes in relative power alter the rational economic decisionmaking process applied by the private decisionmakers. This study supports the proposition that such change would be in the public interest.

NOTES

1. Anil Verma, "Relative Flow of Capital to Union and Nonunion Plants Within a Firm," *Industrial Relations* 24, 3 (Fall 1985) pp. 395-405.

2. See especially *First National Maintenance Corporation v. National Labor Relations Board,* 452 U.S. 666 (1981); and *Otis Elevator Co.*, 269 National Labor Relations Board 891 (1984).

3. Cited in Bureau of National Affairs, *Labor Relations Reporter*, 112 LRR 327 (April 1983).

4. Paul F. Gerhart, "Finding Alternatives to Plant Closing," IRRA Spring Meeting, *Labor Law Journal* (August 1984) pp. 469-474.

5. A discussion of public policy issues with appropriate citations appears in the final portion of this chapter.

6. A 1986 decision by Cleveland Twist Drill to close its Cynthiana, Kentucky plant and consolidate production in Cleveland was the reverse of what usually happens, although Ohio Rubber made a similar decision in 1984 to close southern locations and consolidate production in Cleveland.

7. See Verma, "Relative Flow of Capital," for a more general discussion of this phenomenon.

8. Robert B. McKersie and William S. McKersie, *Plant Closings: What Can Be Learned from Best Practice*, Washington, DC: Government Printing Office.

9. In *Otis Elevator Co.*, however, the National Labor Relations Board held that when a plant closing decision "turns" on labor costs, it is a mandatory subject.

10. See opinion of Justice Blackmun in *First National Maintenance Corp. v. NLRB*.

11. The question of whether advance notice should be required as a matter of law is beyond the purview of this study. Many companies, including several in this study, have voluntarily negotiated into their labor agreements a commitment to notify the union some minimal period of time prior to a closure (or substantial layoff), however, e.g., Goodyear, General Mills.

12. Pursuant to *Allied Chemical and Alkali Workers Local 1 v. Pittsburgh Plate Glass Company*, 404 U.S. 157 (1971), the employer is bound for the term of the contract when it negotiates an agreement on a permissive issue only when the agreement "vitally affects" the employees' terms and conditions of employment.

13. In *Jacobs Manufacturing Company*, 94 NLRB 1214 (1951), enf'd, 196 F.2d 680 (2d cir. 1952), the NLRB established that unilateral changes involving mandatory issues are prohibited. Where the item is "contained in" the contract, no change may be made during the term of the contract, even if the employer has negotiated to impasse with the union. However, if the issue is totally unforeseen and not contained in the contract, unilateral change is possible *after* the parties have negotiated to impasse.